Assessing Neuromotor
for Learning

MW01196879

Assessing Neuromotor Readiness for Learning

The INPP Developmental Screening Test and School Intervention Programme

Author
Sally Goddard Blythe, MSc (Psych), FRSA

Illustrator
Luca Papp

WILEY-BLACKWELL

A John Wiley & Sons, Ltd., Publication

This book is a revised and extended version of: Goddard Blythe (1996) The INPP *Test Battery and Developmental Exercise Programme for use in Schools* produced by The Institute for Neuro-Physiological Psychology (INPP Ltd), Chester, UK.

Wiley-Blackwell is an imprint of John Wiley & Sons, formed by the merger of Wiley's global Scientific, Technical and Medical business with Blackwell Publishing.

Registered Office
John Wiley & Sons Ltd, The Atrium, Southern Gate, Chichester, West Sussex, PO19 8SQ, UK

Editorial Offices
350 Main Street, Malden, MA 02148-5020, USA
9600 Garsington Road, Oxford, OX4 2DQ, UK
The Atrium, Southern Gate, Chichester, West Sussex, PO19 8SQ, UK

For details of our global editorial offices, for customer services, and for information about how to apply for permission to reuse the copyright material in this book please see our website at www.wiley.com/wiley-blackwell.

Library of Congress Cataloging-in-Publication Data

Goddard, Sally, 1957-
   Assessing neuromotor readiness for learning : the INPP developmental screening test and school intervention programme / Sally Goddard Blythe.
        p. cm.
   Includes bibliographical references and index.
   ISBN 978-1-119-97068-2 (pbk.)
   1. Learning disabled children–Education.   2. Learning disabilities–Physiological aspects.
3. Movement disorders in children–Diagnosis.   4. Movement disorders in children–Treatment.
5. Motor ability–Testing. I. Title.
   LC4704.G64 2012
   371.9–dc23

                                                                                  2011043298

A catalogue record for this book is available from the British Library.

Wiley also publishes its books in a variety of electronic formats. Some content that appears in print may not be available in electronic books.

Set in 10/13pt, Scala by Thomson Digital, Noida, India

Contents

Acknowledgements

Sheila Dobie OBE for permission to use examples of exercises developed by her to train bilateral integration.

Riverside Publishing for permission to reproduce figures from the Bender Visual Gestalt test

Ágnes Nyiregyházi Dobrovits and Magdalena Zweegman for arranging revision of all drawings for Chapter 4.

To schools that have participated in The INPP Developmental Movement Programme for Schools, carried out assessments and given permission for their results to be made available for publication.

1
Introduction

NTRODUCTION

▶ 1.1 OVERVIEW

A significant percentage of children in mainstream schools has been found to have immature motor skills and postural instability.[1] Such neuromotor immaturity is often rooted in the continued presence of a cluster of primitive reflexes (normally present in infants up to six months of age, and then replaced over time by postural reactions). Research has shown that there is a direct correlation between immature motor skills and educational achievement. With proper guidance and instruction, teachers and other professionals can be trained to screen for signs of such delay, so that appropriate referrals can be made or physical intervention programmes introduced. This book provides all the tools and guidance needed to identify children with such immaturity, implement a physical programme if appropriate and evaluate outcomes.

There are many motor training and movement programmes available, but the model developed by The Institute for Neuro-Physiological Psychology (INPP) described in this book is unique in having been evaluated in practice and offering a means of assessing neuromotor status in the pre-school and school-aged child both at the beginning and end of intervention.

The book is organized in three sections:

1. The first section offers a series of screening tests for children aged 4–7 years to assess the presence of three reflexes, control of static balance, coordination, visual perception and visual-motor integration.
2. The second section provides a similar series of screening tests for children from seven years of age and above.
3. The third section details a complete developmental movement programme designed to be used with whole classes or smaller groups of children over the course of one academic year.

The book is supported and enhanced by a password-protected INPP video training material and score sheets, available for download to purchasers of the book for a period of one month from www.accessnmr.inpp.org.uk. Additional training courses on how to implement both series of screening tests and the exercise programme are also available from INPP.

Assessing Neuromotor Readiness for Learning: The INPP Developmental Screening Test and School Intervention Programme_, First Edition. Sally Goddard Blythe.
© 2012 John Wiley & Sons, Ltd. Published 2012 by John Wiley & Sons, Ltd.

▶ 1.2 RATIONALE FOR SCREENING AND REMEDIATION OF NEUROMOTOR IMMATURITY

The INPP programme for schools is based on a clinical programme developed at The Institute for Neuro-Physiological Psychology (INPP); it has been used since the 1970s. In 1996, key tests were selected from the INPP full diagnostic assessment and clinical programme and adapted by the author for use with larger groups of children in a school setting.

This adapted series of screening tests is intended to be used by teachers, doctors and other trained professionals involved in child development and education *as a screening tool only*. It will not provide sufficient detailed information to justify a diagnosis, nor is it intended to replace standard neurological examinations, psychological or educational assessments usually carried out by trained psychologists, remedial specialists, medical and other non-medical professionals. It will, however, provide tools which enable a teacher to identify children who are under-achieving as a result of immature neuromotor skills and who are likely to benefit from the INPP programmes or other physical remedial programmes.

The INPP developmental movement programme comprises a series of daily exercises, based on movements normally made by the developing child in the first year of life. These movements must be carried out every day under teacher supervision. One of the major differences between the INPP Programme and many other programmes designed to improve coordination and balance, is that the INPP exercises take children back to the very *beginning* of balance training and postural development.

▶ 1.3 WHAT IS INPP?

The Institute for Neuro-Physiological Psychology (INPP) was established in 1975 by Psychologist Peter Blythe PhD with several aims in mind:

1. To research into the effects of immaturity in the functioning of the central nervous system (CNS) in children with specific learning difficulties (and adults suffering from anxiety states, agoraphobia and panic disorder).
2. To develop reliable methods of assessing CNS maturity.
3. To devise effective remedial intervention programmes.

Children seen at the INPP are examined on an individual basis using a series of standard medical tests to assess a range of physical abilities:

- gross muscle coordination and balance;
- patterns of motor development;
- cerebellar involvement;
- dysdiadochokinesia (ability to carry out rapid alternate movements);
- aberrant primitive and postural reflexes;
- oculomotor functioning (control of eye movements);
- visual perception
- visual motor integration (VMI)
- audiometric examination and dichotic listening.

The diagnostic assessment findings provide the basis for an individual regime of physical exercises which the child carries out every day at home under parental supervision. The exercises take between five and ten minutes a day over a period of approximately twelve months. The child is reviewed at six to eight weekly intervals to assess progress and adjust the exercises accordingly.

One of the problems with the INPP clinical programme has always been that it involves detailed assessment on a one-to-one basis, is costly in terms of professional time and can, therefore, only reach a relatively small number of the children who would benefit from this type of assessment and intervention. It was to overcome this problem that, in 1996, the author selected a reduced number of tests from the INPP diagnostic assessment and compiled the shortened screening tests in this book, which have been designed to be used as a *screening device* by teachers and other professionals involved in education and child development, to enable them to identify children with signs of neuromotor immaturity.[2]

▶ 1.4 THE INPP DEVELOPMENTAL MOVEMENT PROGRAMME FOR SCHOOLS

As part of the same package, the author also devised a unique developmental movement programme for use in schools. The concept behind the combined screening tests and developmental programme was that teachers could be trained in a one day course how to administer the screening tests, enabling them to identify children with signs of neuromotor immaturity in the classroom and implement effective intervention.

The Developmental Movement Programme is designed to be used with a whole class of children or smaller selected groups for ten minutes a day, every school day over the course of one academic year. Teachers do not select specific exercises for individual children but use the developmental movements in sequence, progressing according to the abilities of the class with the slowest child setting the pace.

This programme has been widely used in individual schools throughout the United Kingdom, in other European countries and as far afield as South Africa and Mexico. Research carried out on the screening tests and developmental movement programme has consistently shown that:

1. Neuromotor immaturity is a factor amongst children in mainstream schools.
2. There is a link between neuromotor immaturity and lower educational performance.
3. The INPP Developmental Movement Programme is effective in reducing markers of neuromotor immaturity.
4. When clear signs of neuromotor immaturity (>25%) *and* educational under-achievement coexist, children who followed the INPP developmental movement programme showed greater improvements in measures of non-verbal cognitive performance and reading.[3]
5. Small group studies have indicated that children who were under-achieving by more than a year in reading and who had clear signs of neuromotor immaturity (>50%), made significantly increased gains in reading at the end of the year having followed the INPP Developmental Movement Programme.[4]

▶ 1.5   WHAT IS NEUROMOTOR IMMATURITY?

Neuromotor performance describes a complex functional behaviour which results from activation of the central and peripheral nervous systems and involves motor structures which operate through the musculo-skeletal system involving multiple inputs from the individual's internal and external environment. The systems and structures responsible for movement within an individual are constantly evolving throughout the developmental process, but at certain stages in development a child is expected to have attained a certain level of neuromotor performance. Motor milestones and motor performance provide outward signs of functional neuromotor maturity.

Neuromotor *imm*aturity describes the retention of immature patterns of movement control. These may occur as a result of classical neurological signs (pathology) or be reflective of a functional or developmental delay in the pathways involved. The INPP screening tests are aimed at identifying various 'soft signs'[*] of neurological dysfunction together with the presence of three primitive reflexes in the school-aged population. These tests do not point to causation, neither do they predict learning outcomes in individuals, but they can help to identify the presence of obstacles to educational achievement. Furthermore, in many cases these obstacles can be removed with the use of a specific developmental movement programme.

▶ 1.6   WHAT IS THE SIGNIFICANCE OF PRIMITIVE REFLEXES TO EDUCATION?

Primitive reflexes are included in the INPP screening tests because the presence of primitive reflexes at key stages in development provides acknowledged signposts of maturity in the functioning of the central nervous system. While doctors, midwives and health visitors are familiar with assessment of the primitive reflexes at birth, and tests for primitive reflexes are repeated at developmental check-ups in the first six months of postnatal life, if development appears to be progressing normally in the first year then these tests are not repeated in the pre-school or school-aged child

'While motor milestones – the neurodevelopmental functional end point of the transitioning of the immature and mature primitive reflexes into volitional activity – have been highlighted in predicting future motor function, the primitive reflexes represent the earliest neurodevelopmental markers available for study. By paediatricians becoming familiar with their quantitative and qualitative aspects, coupled with the time of their appearance and suppression, they will have this neuromotor tool available for the early detection of a significant motor handicap. Primitive reflexes have been highlighted since they are available at birth to be clinically evaluated and followed during sequential office visits during the first six months of life, the time during which infants are more closely followed at office visits. Delay or deviancy (non-sequential appearance) of motor milestones are preceded by an exaggeration or delayed suppression of the primitive reflexes'.[5]

---

[*] Soft sign – a mild or slight neurologic abnormality that does not provide specific information about cause or locus of the problem.

▶ 1.7 WHAT ARE PRIMITIVE REFLEXES?

Primitive reflexes are a group of reflexes which develop during life in the womb, are fully developed at birth in the full term baby (40 weeks) and are gradually inhibited and transformed into more mature patterns and postural abilities during the first six months of postnatal life. Only one of the primitive reflexes, the Tonic Labyrinthine Reflex (TLR), can remain in a modified form up to three and a half years of age.

Inhibition and transformation occur primarily as a result of maturation within the developing central nervous system. Primitive reflexes never entirely disappear but become inhibited as 'higher' centres in the brain mature in the first months of life. Primitive reflexes can remain active if there has been damage to higher centres in early life, such as cerebral palsy, or if there is accident or damage to higher brain centres in later life, for example after a stroke, head injury or in degenerative diseases of the central nervous system, such as multiple sclerosis or Alzheimer's disease. According to medical theory, primitive reflexes should not remain active in the general population beyond six months of age, and if elicited beyond this age are usually considered to be indicative of underlying pathology.

However, there is an increasing body of evidence which suggests that *traces* of primitive reflexes (residual reflexes) can remain active in the general population in the absence of identified pathology.[1,3,6–9] These individuals often do not fit into a particular diagnostic category, but the development of certain motor functions necessary to support learning fail to remain commensurate with chronological age. Residual presence of primitive reflexes in children above the age of six months can, therefore, provide indications of neuromotor immaturity, which acts as a barrier to learning.

Assessment of primitive reflexes beyond the first six months of life provides the clinician or educator with tools with which to:

1. Identify signs of neuromotor immaturity (Identification).
2. Assess the type and level of intervention that is appropriate for the child (Intervention/ Remediation).
3. Measure change in reflex status before and after intervention (Evaluation).

▶ 1.8 WHAT IS THE SIGNIFICANCE OF NEUROMOTOR MATURITY TO EDUCATION?

A longitudinal study tracking the progress of nearly fifteen thousand children who were born in the United Kingdom between 2000 and 2001[10] released findings in February 2010; it showed that children who failed at nine months to reach four key milestones in gross motor development relating to sitting unaided, crawling, standing and taking their first steps were found to be five points behind on average cognitive ability tests taken at five years of age compared to those who passed the milestones. 'Delay in gross and fine motor development in a child's first year, was significantly associated with cognitive development and behavioural adjustment at five'.[11]

Readiness for school requires much more than a child simply reaching the chronological age for school entry. To perform well in an educational environment, a child needs to be able to:

sit still, focus attention on one task without being distracted by irrelevant environmental stimuli, hold and manipulate a writing instrument, and to control the eye movements necessary to maintain a stable image on the page, follow a line of print without the eyes 'jumping' or losing their place and adjust visual focus between different distances at speed. These are physical abilities, which are linked to the development and maturation of motor skills and postural control. Growth and physical development are as important to education as they are to the field of developmental medicine but have been largely ignored by the educational system since the routine developmental testing of all children was phased out (in the United Kingdom) in the 1980s.

The disappearance of developmental testing of every child at the time of school entry was the result of two changes in the administration of the whole area of special needs in education in the United Kingdom. First responsibility for the management of special needs was handed over from the Department of Health to the then Department of Education and Science. This meant that responsibility for investigating the causes of special needs transferred from the domain of medicine to that of the educational psychologist and teachers trained in special educational needs. Under this arrangement, although the testing of children's *cognitive* abilities was secure, the testing of children's physical developmental status was no longer carried out as a matter of course. Second in the words of a retired paediatrician 'we entered an era of evidence-based medicine when it became necessary to provide a proven remedy for any problems that were detected as a result of routine testing – at that time we (the medical profession) did not have the resources or a standard effective method of remediation to offer – and the routine developmental testing of every child was phased out'.[12]

One of the outcomes of these changes has been that children who are delayed in specific aspects of their physical development but who have not received a medical diagnosis simply 'slip through the net' of services which should be in place to identify underlying factors and provide appropriate remedial intervention or educational support. These children are at risk of under-achieving at school, not because they lack intelligence or motivation to learn but because some of the physical skills which are needed to support and demonstrate intelligence in the classroom are under-developed. Furthermore, it is often assumed by teachers that such children are performing well enough and, consequently, they are not identified as under-achieving or having a special educational need, 'hovering at just below age expectation achievement'.[13] If underlying problems connected to the development of physical skills are not recognized, these children are at increased risk not only of under-performing but of experiencing frustration and developing associated 'secondary' behavioural signs.

While there can be many reasons for educational under-achievement, 'Factors such as home background, attendance, quality of teaching, socio-psychological interrelationships, learning difficulties etc. all come into play. Not all of these are within the compass of the teacher to easily control and alter. However, neuromotor immaturity is one significant factor that through a programme of therapeutic movement exercises, developed by INPP, schools can do something about'.[13] For some children barriers to learning can be removed with appropriate educational input, but children with neuromotor immaturity are less likely to reap long term benefits from traditional educational responses to under-achievement which include:

- Additional teaching to support the area of deficit combined with further practice of the same.
- Diagnosis of 'specific need teaching' in ways which maximize their learning.
- Providing strategies or accommodations for specific needs in the classroom.

The identification of underlying physical factors opens up the possibility of effective remedial intervention aimed at the specific mechanisms at fault.

The INPP Screening Tests have been compiled to narrow the gap which exists between the professions of medicine, education and psychology in identifying children who have physical barriers to learning. The INPP Developmental Movement Programme has been designed to help children overcome some of these barriers.

▶ 1.9 WHAT IS THE PURPOSE OF DEVELOPMENTAL SCREENING TESTS?

Screening tests are tests which have been developed based on evidence from research which has consistently demonstrated that a cluster of specific symptoms is often linked to specific disorders or dysfunctions.

Screening tests should *not* be used to form a diagnosis, but rather provide professionals with tools to identify individuals who may need more detailed specialist examination or, as indicators for specific types of evaluation or remediation.

Screening tests are *not* meant to replace standard neurological, educational or psychological examinations or assessments carried out by trained professionals, but they *can* help to detect factors which underlie the presenting problems.

The terms 'screening' and 'assessment' are not interchangeable. Screening is a preliminary process for identifying, from all the children, those who may be at risk of future difficulty in school (e.g., inability to meet academic expectations) and those who may have special needs in learning (e.g., extraordinary abilities and talents or handicapping conditions). In both cases, if screening tests yield high scores for indicators of abnormality the child must be referred for assessment to evaluate whether they require treatment for a specific disorder (e.g., visual problem, hearing deficit, motor training, etc.), adaptations of the regular instructional programme, or to discover if they qualify for specialized educational placement.

The INPP screening tests comprise a series of tests compiled from a number of different sources which have been combined to provide a general picture of a *child's neuromotor skills* and *neuromotor readiness* to respond to the demands of formal education. They should not be used as a basis to exclude children from particular activities or year group but are simply intended to provide an indication of a child's neuromotor performance on a range of skills necessary to support cognitive learning in the classroom.

▶ 1.10 WHY ASSESS POSTURE AND BALANCE?

Posture is defined as the reflex anti-gravitational adaptation of a living body to the environment in which he or she lives. Posture depends on reflex acts which occur as a result of the integration of several sensory inputs and rapid adaptive motor reactions, chiefly involving the visual, proprioceptive and vestibular systems. 'Posture means unconscious, inattentive, anti-gravitational adaptation to the environment'.[14] When reflex actions are functioning efficiently and at a developmentally appropriate level, they free 'higher' cognitive systems in the brain from conscious involvement in the maintenance of postural control. Conversely, if reflexes are not functioning in an age-appropriate fashion, then conscious attention must be diverted to the adaptation and maintenance of postural control at the expense of attention to other cognitive tasks. Posture is also essential to support static balance, to provide a frame of reference for coordination and a stable platform for centres involved in the control of eye movements (oculomotor functioning).

▶ 1.11 WHY CARRY OUT ASSESSMENTS FOR BALANCE?

Balance is a continuous dynamic process which describes the interplay between various forces, particularly gravity acting with the motor power of the skeletal muscles. A child has achieved equilibrium when it can maintain and control postures, positions and attitudes.[15] Balance is the end product of cooperation between proprioception, vestibular functioning and vision, mediated by the cerebellum. Posture and balance together provide the bases for motor activities on which all physical aspects of learning depend.

'To have a sense of balance one has to know where one is in space at any particular moment. In vertebrates the point of reference for the balance mechanism is the head. The vestibular system (balance mechanism) informs the brain where the head is in relationship to the external environment. The proprioceptive system informs the brain where the head is in relation to the rest of the body, thus informing it where the head is in relation to its supporting base. Any movement of any part of the body is made with reference to the brain's understanding of where it is in relationship to its structural support (base). With these three inputs the brain can instruct a model of the head and body in relationship to itself and the external world'.[16] Abnormal primitive reflexes in the school-aged child provide evidence of lack of integration in the functioning of these three systems, which are fundamental to the sense of position in space. Problems in control of balance can be manifested in a number of ways:

- Postural control
- Coordination
- Control of eye movements (affecting visual perception)
- Perception – for example vertigo, sense of direction
- Vegetative symptoms – for example nausea, dizziness, disorientation.

Control of balance provides not only physical stability for moving in space but also acts as one of the main reference points for cognitive operations in space, including orientation (knowing your place in space, necessary to navigate through space), directional awareness (needed for way finding, understanding the orientation of symbols, e.g. b and d, p and q, 2 and 5, and being able to read an analogue clock or a compass) and mental operations in space, such as being able to understand that addition and subtraction, multiplication and division are the same processes in reverse.

▶ 1.12 WHAT IS THE DIFFERENCE BETWEEN STATIC BALANCE AND DYNAMIC BALANCE?

Static balance describes postural fixation, which consists of stabilized body attitudes. Static balance is necessary to be able to remain still in fixed positions; children who have poor control of static balance find it difficult to sit or stay still. These children tend to be restless at activities that require remaining in a relatively fixed position, needing to be 'in motion' in order to maintain control of the body. This can be seen as fidgeting when sitting to write or when attending or listening passively but they may have relatively good coordination when engaged in activities which involve action, such as on the sports field.

Some research has pointed to a link between the ability to maintain balance while standing on one leg and specific language disorders.[14]

Dynamic balance describes the various translations and re-adaptations of postural role in performing efficient movements. Children with poorly developed control of dynamic balance will tend to shy away from robust physical activities, or activities which involve translation of position in space – carrying out forward rolls, vaulting over an object – and lack confidence in situations which require rapid adaptive reactions.

1.13 WHAT IS THE SIGNIFICANCE OF POSTURAL CONTROL TO LEARNING?

Posture is not only a neuro-*physiological* function which ensures that physical stability and mobility against the pull of gravity, but it is also 'primarily a central neuro-*psychological* system which embraces a wide range of functional levels from spinal reflexes to higher mental processes'.[17] Postural control is linked to at least three perceptual systems – vestibular (balance), proprioceptive and visual – and dysfunction in any one of these systems or how they operate together can affect the processes of perception on which all higher academic skills depend. Posture both supports and reflects the functional relationship between the brain and the body, to the extent that is has been said that there is nothing in the mind that cannot be seen in the posture.[18]

1.14 PRIMITIVE REFLEXES: WHY HAVE THESE THREE REFLEXES BEEN SELECTED FOR EVALUATION?

Detailed examination of reflex status should only be undertaken by a professional qualified in child development who has undergone specific training in the testing of infant reflexes (doctor, physiotherapist, occupational therapist, INPP trained practitioner, for example). However, for purposes of *education* and *screening*, there are three primitive reflexes that have consistently been shown to act as barriers to learning if they persist in the school-aged child:

1. The Asymmetrical Tonic Neck Reflex (ATNR)
2. The Symmetrical Tonic Neck Reflex (STNR)
3. The Tonic Labyrinthine Reflex (TLR).

1.14.1 THE ASYMMETRICAL TONIC NECK REFLEX (ATNR)

The Asymmetrical Tonic Neck Reflex (ATNR) emerges in normal development at about 18 weeks' gestation, at about the same time as the mother starts to become aware of her baby's movements. Rotation of the head to one side elicits extension of the arm and leg on the side to which the head is turned and retraction of the opposite arm and leg. This reflex increases in strength during the remainder of pregnancy and should be fully developed at birth in a baby born at full term.

In the first months of life the ATNR plays a part in spontaneous movements, developing homolateral (one sided) movements and is one of the earliest mechanisms for training hand-eye coordination. It is normally inhibited between four and six months of age. (Figures 1.1 and 1.2).

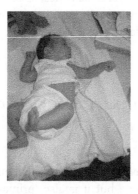

Figure 1.1   ATNR neonate

Figure 1.2   ATNR inhibited about six months

Retention of the ATNR beyond six months of age can interfere with the development of subsequent motor abilities such as rolling over, commando-style crawling, control of upright balance when the head is turned to one side, the ability to cross the midline of the body with affect upon bilateral integration, eye movements and hand–eye coordination. Some observations have indicated a link between retention of the ATNR and failure to develop a preferred side of functioning.[19,20] In the school-aged child, a residual ATNR can interfere with activities which involve crossing the midline, especially control of the hand when writing. If it is present in combination with other reflexes linked to the control of the eye movements needed for reading, it can obstruct reading. Prevalence of the ATNR has been found to be greater in some children with reading difficulties.[8]

1.14.2   THE SYMMETRICAL TONIC NECK REFLEX (STNR)

The Symmetrical Tonic Neck Reflex (STNR) is present for a few days at birth, recedes and re-emerges between five and eight months at about the time the infant is learning to push up on to hands and knees in preparation for crawling. It should only remain active for a short period, as retention can interfere with the next developmental stages of crawling on hands and knees,† sitting and standing posture and hand–eye coordination.

---

† Crawling on hands and knees is sometimes referred to as creeping, particularly in American literature on child development.

The STNR is elicited in a four-point kneeling (quadruped) position. If the head is tilted back (extended) there is an increase in extensor muscle tone in the arms, and flexor tone in the hips and knees (Figure 1.3).

Figure 1.3   STNR in extension

If the head is tilted forward (flexed) it results in an increase in flexor tone in the arms, causing the arms to bend, and extensor tone in the muscles of the hips and knees to increase (Figure 1.4).

Figure 1.4   STNR in flexion

While the STNR has an important function in helping the infant to defy gravity in the first year of life, firstly in getting on to hands and knees, and secondly in helping to pull to standing at the side of the cot, playpen or an item of furniture, it should not persist in the quadruped position after the child has learned to get on to hands and knees, or in the upright position once the child has learned to stand unaided. If it fails to be suppressed, distribution of muscle tone in the upper and lower halves of the body is affected by the position of the head.

In the school-aged child this can be most readily observed in sitting posture when writing. When the child looks down at the writing surface, the arms want to be bend (and the legs extend), making the child lean further towards the writing surface, so that in some cases the child may end up almost lying on the desk to write (Figure 1.5). In this case, when the head is raised he/she can sit up, but each time he/she looks down the arms bend. If he/she extends her head the opposite reaction occurs – the arms straighten and the legs bend.

Figure 1.5   Sitting posture typical of an STNR in flexion

In addition to making sitting awkward and uncomfortable, retention of the STNR in the school-aged child can also affect specific hand–eye coordination skills, such as those needed to bring the hand to the mouth when eating. Children with a residual STNR are often messy eaters who find it difficult to bring a fork, spoon or cup to the mouth without spilling some of the contents on the way. It can also interfere with the development of specific oculomotor skills, such as speed of accommodation (the ability to adjust focus between different visual distances) needed to copy from the board or track an object approaching at speed (catching a ball for example), and the vertical tracking skills needed to align columns correctly in maths[21] and to judge heights.

1.14.3   THE TONIC LABYRINTHINE REFLEX (TLR)

The Tonic Labyrinthine Reflex (TLR) is present at birth and is a primitive reaction to gravity which recedes as head control, muscle tone and postural control develop. When the newborn is held in the supine position, if the head is lowered below the level of the spine the arms and legs will extend; if the head is raised above the level of the spine the arms and legs will flex. As head righting reflexes develop in the first weeks and months after birth, the TLR diminishes to be replaced by a series of more advanced postural reactions which facilitate correction of head position in response to movement of the body or the environment. These automatic head righting reactions provide the basis not only for control of balance and general coordination but also a stable platform for the control of eye movements.

Retention of the TLR beyond three and a half years of age is associated with problems with balance, muscle tone, control of the eye movements needed for reading, writing, copying and maths, and can also affect spatial skills. This is because spatial awareness and the ability to manoeuvre and carry out cognitive operations in space depend first on having a secure physical reference point in space.

▶ 1.15   WHAT EVIDENCE IS THERE LINKING BALANCE, POSTURE AND REFLEXES TO EDUCATIONAL ACHIEVEMENT?

The concept that neurological dysfunction can underlie problems with learning is not new. Neither is the theory that the use of interventions designed to ameliorate neurological dysfunction can improve learning outcomes.

Developmental disabilities were recognized in the nineteenth century chiefly as two forms of delay – cognitive delay in the case of mental retardation and motor delay in the case of cerebral palsy – but less severe symptoms involving discrepancy between intelligence and more specialized areas of language, learning, communication and social interaction, including early infant autism, only emerged in the twentieth century.

In the 1920s the French were among the first to notice a link between 'motor awkwardness' and learning disabilities,[22] which they sometimes described as 'psychomotor syndromes'. In 1940, R. S. Paine described the presence of several isolated motor signs, such as awkwardness, tremor, hyperreflexia or mild impairments in walking, in children with specific learning difficulties. He also pointed to problems in the perception of auditory or visual information, faulty concepts of space, diminished attention span, difficulty in abstract thinking and delays in academic achievement being characteristic features of children with learning disabilities. Mild epileptic symptoms were also noted as sometimes being present.[23]

In other countries the term minimal brain dysfunction (MBD) started to be used. MBD was formally defined in 1966 by Samuel Clements as a combination of average or above average intelligence with certain mild-to-severe learning or behavioural disabilities characterizing deviant functioning of the central nervous system, which could involve impairments in visual or auditory perception, conceptualization, language and memory, and difficulty controlling attention, impulses and motor function,[24] but with more than 99 possible symptoms listed as diagnostic criteria for MBD by the 1970s the term MBD was already being rejected as being too broad.

Retention of primitive reflexes as one of the signs of cerebral palsy has long been recognized. In cerebral palsy retention of the reflexes occurs as a result of damage to the brain or abnormal development, which may have occurred prenatally, at birth or postnatally (Bobath and Bobath,[25,26] Illingworth,[27] Capute and Accardo,[28] Fiorentino,[29] Levitt,[30] Brunnström[31]). In cerebral palsy damage to the immature brain interferes with the normal process of maturation in a predictable, orderly, developmental sequence, resulting in lack of inhibition, demonstrated by prolonged retention of the primitive undifferentiated patterns of movement control characteristic of infancy, accompanied by abnormal muscle tone, development of postural control, impaired patterns of movement and delayed motor development. For many years it was assumed that retention of primitive reflexes could not exist to any lesser degree in the absence of identified pathology and, therefore, primitive reflexes were not the subject of investigation in children with less severe motor delays or signs of a specific learning difficulty.

Investigations into the presence of abnormal or immature reflexes in individuals with specific learning difficulties emerged from various schools of thought in the 1970s. In 1970, an occupational therapist at the University of Kansas, USA, carried out a study in which she compared the reflex levels of a group of neurologically impaired children with a group of children with no known neurological impairment. Every one of the group diagnosed with neurological impairment had abnormal reflexes. Eight out of nineteen subjects in the 'normal' or comparison group also showed some reflex abnormalities and it was subsequently found that of these eight, one had behaviour problems and the remainder had either reading and/or writing problems.[32]

In the same year, also at the University of Kansas, Barbara Rider, Rider, another occupational therapist, set out to assess the prevalence of abnormal reflex responses in normal second grade children, comparing their results to a group of learning disabled children. She found that the learning disabled children had significantly more abnormal reflex responses than the normal children. Using the Wide Range Achievement Test (WRAT) scores as an independent measure, she compared WRAT scores on the basis of whether there were abnormal reflex responses or not. Children with integrated reflexes scored consistently higher on the achievement tests than those with abnormal reflexes.[33]

In 1976 at the University of Purdue, USA, Miriam Bender examined the effect of just one reflex, the Symmetrical Tonic Neck Reflex (STNR) on education, and found that the STNR was present in 75% of a group of learning disabled children but not present in *any* of a comparison group of children who had no history of learning disabilities. She also developed a series of exercises designed to help inhibit the STNR, and observed that many of the children's presenting symptoms improved.[34]

In 1978, Ayres, the creator of Sensory Integration (SI) therapy, observed that one of the major symptoms manifested by children in disorders of postural and bilateral integration was 'poorly developed primitive postural reflexes, immature equilibrium reactions, poor ocular control and deficits in a variety of subtle parameters that are related to the fact that man is a bilateral and symmetrical being'.[35] One of the aims of sensory integration therapy was, 'not to teach specific skills such as matching visual stimuli, learning to remember a sequence of sounds, differentiating one sound from another, drawing lines from one point to another, or even the basic academic material. Rather, the objective is to enhance the brain's ability to learn *how* to do these things'.[35] The objective was modification of the neurological dysfunction interfering with learning rather than attacking the symptoms of the dysfunction.

In 1994, Wilkinson carried out a replica of Rider's 1970 study. She found not only a link between residual primitive reflexes and specific learning difficulties, but also identified a connection between residual primitive reflexes and educational under-achievement. Her findings indicated that one reflex – the Tonic Labyrinthine Reflex (TLR) – underpinned many of the presenting educational difficulties and that there was a relationship between the continued presence of the Moro reflex and specific problems with mathematics.[36]

Goddard Blythe and Hyland in 1997 investigated differences in the early development of 72 children diagnosed with specific learning difficulties compared to children with no evidence of specific learning difficulty using the INPP Screening Questionnaire.[37–39] They found significant differences in the developmental histories between the two groups, with children in the specific learning difficulty group having a much higher incidence of early life events or signs of delay in motor and language development and factors related to the functioning of the immune system. Delays in learning to walk and talk were particularly significant in the group with specific learning difficulties.[40]

Other studies which have investigated the persistence of abnormal reflexes in children with specific reading difficulties have found the Asymmetrical Tonic Neck Reflex (ATNR) to be present in children with reading difficulties,[6,8,41] a cluster of abnormal primitive and postural reflexes present in a sample of children diagnosed with dyslexia[7] and in children with attention deficit disorder.[42]

Investigations into the incidence of abnormal primitive reflexes in a sample of 672 children in seven mainstream schools in Northern Ireland between 2003 and 2004 revealed that 48% of children aged 5–6 years (P2) and 35% of children aged 8–9 years (P5) still had traces of primitive reflexes; 15% (49) of P5 children had a reading age below their chronological age. Of these, 28 also had elevated levels of retained reflexes. Elevated levels of retained reflexes were correlated with poor educational achievement at baseline. In the younger group (P2) it was found that retained reflexes were correlated with poor cognitive development, poor balance, and teacher assessment of poor concentration/coordination. Neurological scores and teacher assessment at baseline predicted poorer reading and literacy scores at the end of the study.[3]

Some research suggests that children growing up in areas of social disadvantage may also be at greater risk of educational under-achievement, not only as the result of lack of appropriate stimulation in terms of opportunity for language development and reading, but also because of immature motor skills.[43] Empirical findings also suggest a link between neuromotor immaturity, as defined by the continued presence of primitive reflexes, and some behavioural problems in children.[44]

▶ 1.16 WHAT EVIDENCE IS THERE THAT INTERVENTION IN THE FORM OF MOVEMENT PROGRAMMES AIMED AT THE LEVEL OF PRIMITIVE REFLEXES IMPROVES EDUCATIONAL OUTCOMES?

Remediation of educational difficulties tends to be primarily aimed at treating the symptom, that is, focusing resources on teaching and practise of more reading, more writing, more spelling and more maths as is considered necessary. While this can be beneficial if the problem is a direct result of deficit in teaching or the learning of foundation skills, it will not ameliorate difficulties which arise as a result of defects in underlying physical skills which support higher aspects of learning.

The concept of using motor training programmes to improve learning is not new either. Kephart,[45] Frostig,[46] Getman,[47] Cratty,[48] Barsch,[49] Ayres,[35] Belgau,[50] Kiphard and Schilling[51] and others all advocated and developed perceptual and developmental screening and training programmes to improve the perceptual-motor skills of young children to enhance learning outcomes. In 1979 Blythe and McGlown[37] developed the INPP programme for use with individual children; it was aimed specifically at inhibiting primitive reflexes and stimulating the development of more mature postural reactions. A body of research into the effects of intervention programmes aimed at integrating primitive and postural reactions has gradually accumulated over the last 30 years, beginning with small-scale independent studies which have indicated, first, that primitive reflexes can and do respond to specific physical interventions and, second, that maturation in reflex status is accompanied by improvements in coordination and educational measures.[6,52,53]

In 1996, the INPP clinical programme was adapted for use in schools. Research carried out on this programme has consistently shown:

1. There is a significant decrease in active primitive reflexes and improvement in measures of balance and coordination in children who followed the programme compared to control and comparison groups.
2. There are improvements in drawing and reading in children who had both abnormal reflexes and who were performing below chronological age in these skills before introduction of the programme.[54–57]
3. Empirical evidence provided by reports from teachers and head teachers indicates that there are improvements in behaviour,[58] particularly playground behaviour, children are quicker to settle at lessons following the exercises and there are noticeable differences in children's poise and posture.
4. In one study carried out in Northumberland, UK, five children had been referred to the Behavioural Support Service in the area. At the end of the first term on the programme, all of the children were removed from the support service's list despite the fact that no specific behavioural intervention had been given in the intervening time.[58]
5. A follow up study carried out in Germany two years after a cohort of children had completed the school programme found that the participants had maintained the gains they had made two years after they had completed the programme.[59]

The INPP tests and developmental exercises have been developed based upon evidence which has consistently showed that:

1. There is a relationship between children's neuromotor skills and performance on motor-dependent tasks.

2. Maturity in the functioning of the central nervous system may be inferred from children's neuromotor skills.
3. Residual primitive reflexes respond to the INPP developmental exercise programme.
4. Improvement in neuromotor skills can have a positive influence on learning outcomes.

Factors assessed in the INPP screening tests:

- Balance
- Proprioception
- Primitive reflexes: ATNR, STNR and TLR
- Oculomotor functioning (convergence, fixation, saccades)
- Auditory recognition of visual symbols
- Visual perception
- Visual integration
- Visual-motor integration
- Spatial awareness

▶ 1.17 HOW TO USE THE SCREENING TESTS

The following screening tests are intended for use by teachers, doctors and other professionals involved in the development and education of children from five years of age.

The tests are for screening purposes only and should not be used as the basis of a diagnosis, but they may be used to:

1. Identify children with neuromotor immaturity and related difficulties.
2. Identify children likely to benefit from the INPP Developmental Movement Programme for use in Schools.
3. Identify children who have issues related to neuromotor immaturity, visual-perceptual problems or auditory processing deficits who should be referred on for more specialized assessment, diagnosis and intervention.
4. Provide a system of evaluating progress following use of The INPP Developmental Movement Programme for use in Schools and for the evaluation of the other intervention programmes.

While the screening tests may be used as separate items for purposes of identification and evaluation, The INPP Developmental Movement Programme should *only* be used following assessment using the age-appropriate screening tests. The screening tests may be used before and after intervention to evaluate progress.

▶ REFERENCES

[1] Goddard Blythe, SA (2005) Releasing educational potential through movement. A summary of individual studies carried out using the INPP test battery and developmental exercise Programme for use in schools with children with special needs. *Child Care in Practice*, 11(4):415–432.
[2] Goddard Blythe, SA (1996) The INPP test battery and developmental movement programme for use in schools with children with special needs. Restricted publication. INPP Ltd, Chester, UK.

[3] North Eastern Education and Library Board (NEELB) (2004) An evaluation of the pilot INPP movement programme in primary schools in the North Eastern Education and Library Board Northern Ireland. Final Report. Prepared by Brainbox Research Ltd for the NEELB. www.neelb.org.uk.

[4] Fry, J (2010) The INPP Exercise Club – Observations. St John's C of E Primary School, Reading Berkshire, UK. Cited in: Neuro-motor maturity as an indicator of developmental readiness for education. Report on the use of a Neuro-Motor Test Battery and Developmental Movement Programme in Schools in Northumberland and Berkshire. Paper presented at The Institute for Neuro-Physiological Psychology Conference 11–12 April 2010, Miami, FL.

[5] Capute, AJ (1986) Early neuromotor reflexes in infancy. *Pediatr Ann.*, **15**(3): 217, 221–223, 226.

[6] McPhillips, M, Hepper, PG and Mulhern, G (2000) Effects of replicating primary reflex movements on specific reading difficulties in children: a randomised, double-blind, controlled trial. *The Lancet*, **355**: 537–541.

[7] Goddard Blythe, SA (2001) Neurological dysfunction as a significant factor in children diagnosed with dyslexia. Proceedings of the 5th International BDA Conference, April 2001, University of York, UK.

[8] McPhillips, M and Sheehy, N (2004) Prevalence of persistent primary reflex and motor problems in children with reading difficulties. *Dyslexia*, **10**: 316–338.

[9] Holley, PA (2011) Why do some children learn more easily than others? Physical factors influencing effective learning. Med Thesis submitted to Melbourne Graduate School of Education, University of Melbourne, Australia.

[10] Hansen, K, Josh, IH and Dex, S (eds) (2010) *Children of the 21st century. The first five years.* The Policy Press, Bristol, UK.

[11] Schoon, I (2010) Personal communication.

[12] Paynter, A (2004) Learn to move, move to learn. DVD. Learning Through Sharing Publication Series, St Aidan's School Sport Partnership. www.youthsporttrust.org.

[13] Griffin, P (2010) NDD. One barrier to learning that can be removed. Report prepared for INPP and Head of Learning Support and Innovation, Walsall Children's Services – SERCO, Walsall, UK.

[14] King, LJ and Schrager, O (1999) A sensory cognitive approach to the assessment and remediation of developmental learning and behavioural disorders. Symposium sponsored by Continuing Education Programs of America, March 1999, Atlanta, GA.

[15] De Quiros, JL and Schrager, O (1979) *Neurophysiological fundamentals in learning disabilities.* Academic Therapy Publications, Novato, CA.

[16] Teale, M (2011) Explain how certain reflexes can affect control of balance. Essay submitted to The Institute for Neuro-Physiological Psychology. Chester, UK.

[17] Kohen-Raz, R (1996) *Learning disabilities and postural control.* Freund Publishing House, London.

[18] Kohen-Raz, R (2002) Postural Development and School Readiness. Paper presented at The European Conference of Neuro-Developmental Delay in Children with Specific Learning Difficulties, 10 March 2002, Chester, UK.

[19] Gesell, A and Ames, LB (1947) The development of handedness. *Journal of Genetic Pyschology*, **70**: 155–175.

[20] Telleus, C (1980) En komparativ studie av neurologisk skillnader hos born medoch utan Isoch skrivovarigheter. Göteborg Universitet Pyschologisker Instituktionen.

[21] Bein-Wierzibinski, W (2001) Persistent primitive reflexes in elementary school children. Effect on oculomotor and visual perception. Paper presented at The 13th European Conference of Neuro-Developmental Delay in Children with Specific Learning Difficulties, Chester, UK.

[22] Dupre, E (1925) Debilite motrice. In: E. Dupre, *Pathologie de l'Imagination et de l'Emotivie.* Payot, Paris.

[23] De Quiros, JL and Schrager, O (1979) *Neurophysiological fundamentals in learning disabilities.* Academic Therapy Publications, Novato, CA. pp. 146–147.

[24] Clements, SD (1966) Task force one: Minimal brain dysfunction in children. National Institute of Neurological Diseases and Blindness. Monograph No. 3. US Department of Health, Education and Welfare.

[25] Bobath, K and Bobath, B (1955) Tonic reflexes and righting reflexes in diagnosis and assessment of cerebral palsy. *Cerebral Palsy Review*, **16**(5): 3–10, 26.

[26] Bobath, K (1980) *A neurophysiological basis for the treatment of cerebral palsy.* Blackwell Publishing Ltd, Oxford.

[27] Illingworth, RS (1962) *An introduction to developmental assessment in the first year.* National Spastics Society/William Heinemann (Medical Books), London.

[28] Capute, AJ and Accardo, PJ (1991) Cerebral palsy. The spectrum of motor dysfunction. In: Capute, AJ and Accardo, PJ (eds), *Developmental disabilities in infancy and early childhood.* Paul Brookes Publishing Co., Baltimore, MD.

[29] Fiorentino, MR (1981) *Reflex testing methods for evaluating C.N.S. development.* Charles C Thomas, Springfield, IL.

[30] Levitt, S (1977) *Treatment of cerebral palsy and motor delay.* Blackwell Publishing Ltd, Oxford.

[31] Brunnström, S (1970) *Movement therapy in hemiplegia: a neuro-physiological approach.* Harper and Row, New York.

[32] Gustafsson, D (1970) A comparison of basic reflexes with the subtests of the Purdue perceptual-motor survey. Master's thesis, University of Kansas.

[33] Rider, B (1972) Relationship of postural reflexes to learning disabilities. *American Journal of Occupational Therapy,* 26(5): 239–243.

[34] Bender, ML (1976) *Bender—Purdue reflex test.* Academic Therapy Publications, San Rafael, CA.

[35] Ayres, AJ (1978) *Sensory integration and learning disorders.* Western Psychological Services, Los Angeles, CA.

[36] Wilkinson, G (1994) The relationship of primitive postural reflexes to learning difficulty and underachievement. Med thesis. University of Newcastle-upon-Tyne, UK.

[37] Blythe, P and McGlown, D (1979) *An organic basis for neuroses and educational difficulties.* Insight Publications, Chester, UK.

[38] Goddard Blythe, SA (2008) *What babies and children really need.* Hawthorn Press, Stroud, UK.

[39] Goddard Blythe, SA (2009) *Attention, balance and coordination. The A.B.C. of learning success.* John Wiley & Sons Ltd, Chichester.

[40] Goddard Blythe, SA and Hyland, D (1998) Screening for neurological dysfunction in the specific learning difficulty child. *The British Journal of Occupational Therapy,* 10: 459–464.

[41] McPhillips, M and Jordan-Black, J-A (2007) Primary reflex persistence in children with reading difficulties (dyslexia): A cross-sectional study. *Neuropsychologia,* 45: 748–754

[42] Taylor, M, Hougton, S and Chapman, E (2004) Primitive reflexes and Attention Deficit Disorder: Developmental origins of classroom dysfunction. *International Journal of Special Education,* 19: 1.

[43] McPhillips, M and Jordan-Black, J-A (2007) The effect of social disadvantage on motor development in young children: a comparative study. *Journal of Child Psychology and Psychiatry,* 48(12): 1214–1222.

[44] Goddard Blythe, SA (2010) Neuromotor immaturity as an indicator of developmental readiness for education. Paper presented at The Institute for Neuro-Physiological Psychology International Conference, Miami, FL. April 2010.

[45] Kephart, NC (1960) *The slow learner in the classroom.* Charles E Merrill Books Inc., Columbus, OH.

[46] Frostig, M and Horne, D (1964) *The Frostig program for the development of visual perception.* Follett, Chicago, IL.

[47] Getman, G, Kane, E, Halgren, M and McKee, G (1964) *The physiology of readiness: An action program for the development of perception in children.* Programs to Develop School Success, Minneapolis, MN.

[48] Cratty, R (1973) *Teaching motor skills.* Prentice Hall, Englewood Cliffs, NJ.

[49] Barsch, R (1965) A movigenic curriculum. (Bulletin 25). Department of Instruction, Bureau for the Handicapped, Madison, WI.

[50] Belgau, F, (2010) *A life in balance. Discovery of a learning breakthrough.* Outskirts Press Incorporated, Denver, CO.

[51] Kiphard, EJ and Schilling, F (1974) Body Coordination Test for Children (BCT). Beltz Test GMBH, Weinheim, West Germany.

[52] Bernhardsson, K and Davidson, K (1989) Ett Annorlundo sätt att hjälpa med inlärningssvårigheter. The Educational Psychology Department, Gothenburg Education Authority, Sweden.

[53] Bein-Wierzbinski, W, (2001) Persistent primitive reflexes in elementary school children. Effect on oculomotor and visual perception (exercises based on INPP programme). Paper presented at The 13th European Conference of Neuro-Developmental Delay in Children with Specific Learning Difficulties.

[54] Pettman, H (2001) The effects of developmental exercise movements on children with persistent primary reflexes and reading difficulties: A controlled trial. Mellor Primary School, Leicester. Final Report: Best Practice Research Scholarship Study. Department of Education and Skills.

[55] Preedy, P, O'Donovon, C, Scott, J and Wolinski, R (2000) *Exercises for learning*. A Beacon Project between Knowle CE Primary School and Kingsley Preparatory School, Department for Education, UK.

[56] Micklethwaite, J (2004) A report of a study into the efficacy of the INPP School Programme at Swanwick Primary School, Derby. A controlled study of 90 children. Department for Education and Employment Best Practice Scholarship web site: www.teachernet.gov.uk/bprs.

[57] Hunter, P (2004) The effectiveness of a developmental programme designed to be used in with children with special needs. MA Thesis, University of Middlesex, UK.

[58] Marlee, R (2006) Personal communication.

[59] Jändling, M (2003). The use of the INPP movement programme at a German primary school. Paper presented at The 15th European Conference of Neuro-Developmental Delay. Kiel-Oslo-Kiel.

2

Developmental Screening Tests for Use with Children Aged 4–7 Years

▶ 2.1   GENERAL INSTRUCTIONS

All tests have been adapted to comply with regulations (in the United Kingdom) that teachers should if possible avoid physical contact with children in their care.

Testing should be carried out with the child wearing loose clothing and in bare feet.

To ensure that the child has understood verbal instructions correctly, the tester should also demonstrate the beginning of each test procedure.

Additional notes of observations made during tests should be recorded on the separate observation sheets provided and attached to the score sheet.

Please note that certain tests are only developmentally appropriate from five or six years of age. Omit tests where it states that the developmental norm for the test is older than the age of the child being assessed, unless it states that the test may be used for *qualitative* purposes at a younger age.

Qualitative observations enable the tester to observe the quality of performance. This can be re-assessed at a later date or following intervention to observe whether there has been significant change in the quality of performance over time.

Video examples of all test positions, observations and scoring may be found at XXXX. Registration on this web site will enable one month's free access to the training video.

2.1.1   SCORING

All tests are scored using a 5-point rating scale:

0. no abnormality detected (NAD)
1. 25% dysfunction
2. 50% dysfunction
3. 75% dysfunction
4. 100% dysfunction

Assessing Neuromotor Readiness for Learning: The INPP Developmental Screening Test and School Intervention Programme, First Edition. Sally Goddard Blythe.
© 2012 John Wiley & Sons, Ltd. Published 2012 by John Wiley & Sons, Ltd.

Neuromotor tests
1. The Romberg Test
2. One leg stand
3. Creeping on hands and knees
4. Crossing the midline (1)
5. Crossing the midline (2)
6. Finger and thumb opposition test

Tests for primitive reflexes
7. Quadruped test for the Asymmetrical Tonic Neck Reflex (ATNR)
8. Quadruped test for the Symmetrical Tonic Neck Reflex (STNR)
9. Erect test for the Tonic Labyrinthine Reflex (TLR)

Tests for visual perception and visual-motor integration
10. Paper and pencil tests
11. Additional measures

▶ 2.2 NEUROMOTOR TESTS

2.2.1 THE ROMBERG TEST

A test developed by German physician Moritz H. Romberg (1795–1873) to assess proprioception and control of static balance. It provides an indication of loss of the sense of position if the patient loses balance when standing erect, feet together, and eyes closed. By the age of four years a child is expected to be able to perform the Romberg Test without loss of balance for eight seconds with the eyes open and closed.

While a 'positive' Romberg sign is generally considered to be loss of balance on this test, *qualitative* assessment of a child's stability when standing in this position can also be useful in providing indications of immature balance and/or proprioception.

The ability to perform the Romberg Test has been considered an important milestone in postural maturation, and links with another developmental marker, the suppression of synkinetic* movements in the hands and fingers of the contralateral hand when the child is asked to carry out the thumb and finger opposition test.[1]

2.2.1.1 Test Procedure – Romberg Test

Test position – standing.

Standing up straight, feet together, arms and hands to the side, looking straight ahead (Figure 2.1).

Eyes open

The child is instructed to continue looking straight ahead without moving. This position should be maintained for approximately eight seconds.

---

* Synkinesia – the performing of an unintended movement when making a voluntary one; sometimes described as 'overflow' movements.

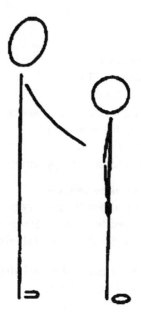

Figure 2.1   Test position for the Romberg Test

Eyes closed

He or she is then asked to maintain the position, but to close the eyes and 'imagine' – pretend – that he/she is looking straight ahead. Hold that position for approximately eight seconds.

2.2.1.2   Observations

Eyes open

- Does the child sway?
- If so, in which direction – backwards, forwards, to the left or right side, or in a circular movement?
- How much does he/she sway?
- Do one or both arms move out and away from the body?
- Does the child's face become contorted or is there 'tongue thrust'?
- Does the child lose his/her balance?

Eyes closed

Note all of the above, paying particular attention to the degree of difficulty outlined above.

2.2.1.3   Scoring for Eyes Open and Eyes Closed

0. None of the observations are noted.
1. Slight sway in any direction: slight movement of the arms away from the body, slight face or tongue involvement.
2. More marked sway: more marked movement of the arms away from the body, and a more marked facial or tongue involvement.
3. Near loss of balance: need to extend the arms to maintain balance.
4. Body involvement led to loss of balance: facial grimaces.

(Please note that a positive score is referred to as a positive Romberg sign. A score of 0 is referred to as a negative Romberg sign).

2.2.2   ONE LEG STAND

The one leg stand test assesses control of static balance and the ability to control balance using one side of the body independently of the other.

In addition to maintaining control of balance while standing on one leg, Schrager[2] demonstrated that observations of both timing and body position while carrying out the one leg stand can provide additional information about maturity of the central nervous system. He found significant differences in the performance of language impaired individuals compared with a group with normal language ability on this test, surmising that the ability to control balance when standing on one leg and language ability may be linked.[3]

2.2.2.1   Test Procedure – One Leg Stand

Test position – standing.

Instruct the child to stand on one leg and to, 'maintain this position as long as you can'. Time (in seconds) the length of time the child can maintain the position without loss of balance or placing the other foot on the ground. This test is performed with **eyes open** (Figure 2.2).

Figure 2.2   Test position for the one leg stand test

2.2.2.2   Developmental Norms[4]

Developmental norms for this test vary between different sources. Some sources state 15 seconds at six years of age and 20 seconds at seven years of age. Others list the scale shown below.

3 years	2 seconds
4 years	4–8 seconds
5 years	8 seconds using either foot
6 years	20 seconds left or right
(8 years	30 seconds right or left)

2.2.2.3 Observations

Inability to stand on one leg for the age appropriate number of seconds may suggest underlying vestibular/postural immaturity, in presenting difficulties and/or difficulty in controlling one side of the body independently from the other.

Also note any marked compensatory or 'overflow' movements of the arms, opposite leg, mouth or hands when carrying out this test.

2.2.2.4 Scoring

0. No abnormality detected.
1. 2 seconds less than normal time in seconds for age of child.
2. 4 seconds less than normal time in seconds for age of child.
3. 6 seconds less than normal time for age of child.
4. 8 seconds or more less than normal time for age of child.

2.2.3 THE CRAWLING ON HANDS AND KNEES TEST

There are four stages a child might pass through in learning to crawl on hands and knees in the first year of life:

1. Homologous – using upper and lower body only; no left/right involvement.
2. Homolateral – reaching with the arm and pushing with the leg on the same side.
3. Unsynchronized cross pattern – using the opposite arm and leg but with no synchrony in the timing of movements in the upper and lower sections of the body.
4. Synchronized cross pattern – opposite arm and leg with movements of the upper and lower body synchronized.

2.2.3.1 Test Procedure – Crawling on Hands and Knees

Test position – hands and knees, as in Figure 2.3.

Figure 2.3   Test position for crawling on hands and knees test (quadruped 'table' position).

Ask the child to lift his/her head up and look at a sighting object at eye level, followed by the instruction:

'I would like you to slowly creep (crawl) forwards on your hands and knees, whilst looking straight ahead all the time, until you reach me. Then turn around and slowly creep back to where you started.'

2.2.3.2 Observations

- Does the child go forward using small 'bunny-rabbit' jumps (homologous)?
- Does the child creep forward use the arm and leg on the same side (homolateral)?
- If cross pattern (opposite arm and leg), is the timing of the movements in the upper and lower body synchronized?
- Does the child rotate the position of one or both hands to 'quarter to, or past the hour'?
- Does the child creep forward with the fingers on one or both hands raised and extended, that is, on fingertips?
- Does the child creep using his/her hands as fists?
- Do one or both feet leave the floor?

2.2.3.3 Scoring

0. None of the observations were noted.
1. One of the observations were noted.
2. Two of the observations were noted.
3. Three were noted.
4. Four were noted.

2.2.4 CROSSING THE MIDLINE, TEST NO. 1

A child should be able to carry out tasks which involve crossing the midline of the body by four years of age.[5–8] Crossing over the midline is important not only for general coordination but for the ability to draw shapes and form letters and numbers.

2.2.4.1 Test Procedure – Crossing the Midline (1)

Test position – standing.

Instruct the child to stand with feet together. If this is too difficult then the heels should be together or touching; arms straight down at the sides of the body.

Instruct the child to bend the elbow so that the forearm and hand are at a 90° angle from the upper arm, which remains straight down from the shoulders and alongside the chest.

Turn the palm of the hand up towards the ceiling with the fingers extended.

Place a hand-sized ball or bean bag in the palm of one hand (Figure 2.4).

Demonstrate passing the object from one hand to the other *across* the midline.

Instruct the child to return to the original test position placing the ball in the opposite hand and then pass the ball slowly back into the other hand.

Repeat this 'crossing the midline' four times.

The tester stands in front of the child while he/she undertakes this test.

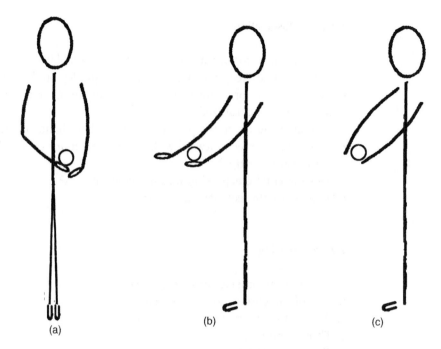

Figure 2.4a, 2.4b and 2.4c Test position and procedures for crossing the midline test (1)

2.2.4.2 Observations

- As the child crosses the midline to put the ball into the opposite palm, note whether the child has difficulty crossing the midline.
- Does the child have to bring the other hand to the midline to take the ball?
- Does he/she find it so difficult that the ball is dropped?
- As the child repeats the task, does his/her balance become impaired, and, if so, to what degree?

2.2.4.3 Scoring

0. None of the above observations were noted.
1. There was a slight hesitation as one or both hands crossed the midline. Note any slight sway in balance as the child carries out the task.
2. There was a definite difficulty as one hand or the other tried to cross the midline. Note any increased sway in balance as the child carries out the task.
3. The child transfers the object to the other hand *at* the midline. Also note if balance is impaired as the child carries out the task and on which side, or if there is 'overflow' in carrying out the movement with the tongue moving in the same direction as the hand, or the eyes converging at the midline.
4. The task was impossible and/or total loss of balance.

2.2.5 CROSSING THE MIDLINE, TEST NO. 2

2.2.5.1 Test Procedure – Crossing the Midline (2)

Test position – standing.

Stand with the feet together and heels together. Ask the child to lift up the right arm (or left arm if the child appears to be left handed), and cross it over the top of the head to touch the lobe of the opposite ear (Figure 2.5).

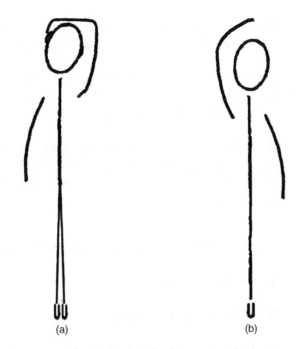

(a)   (b)

Figure 2.5a and 2.5b   Test position and procedures for crossing the midline test (2)

The arms and hand then return to the start position, and the opposite arm and hand repeat the same manoeuvre.

The tester should demonstrate the test to the child before testing.

2.2.5.2   Observations

- Does the child have difficulty with one or both hands/arms crossing the midline?
- Is the whole body involved in the hand/arm movement?
- Does the child make facial or tongue movements?
- Is balance impaired?

2.2.5.3   Scoring

0. None of the above observations were noted.
1. There was slight difficulty in one or both hands crossing the midline over the top of the head. A slight sway, facial and/or body movement.
2. There was a definite difficulty in one or both arms crossing the midline and/or more marked sway or facial and/or body movement.
3. Difficulty in crossing the midline resulted in near loss of balance and very marked body involvement.
4. The task was impossible to complete.

2.2.6   FINGER AND THUMB OPPOSITION TEST

By 38 months of age a child should be able to oppose the thumb to each of the four fingers of the same hand in succession.[9,10] This ability improves between three and eight years of age, although some mirroring of movement may still be observed up to ten years of age.[11] Difficulty in touching the thumb with the fingers of the same hand in systematic succession may be indicative of minor cerebellar dysfunction. Satz *et al.* (1978) demonstrated that difficulty with thumb and finger opposition was among one of the strongest predictors of learning disabilities in the first years of primary (elementary) school.[12]

Qualitative assessment using this test is suitable for use with children from $5^1/_2$ to 6 years of age. Difficulties with thumb and finger opposition will contribute to difficulty with writing and are often found in children with a history of delayed speech.

The ability to suppress synergetic (mirroring movements on the opposite side of the body) improves rapidly between the ages of five and seven years and reflects the ability to act independently with each side of the body, which is considered to be a necessary starting point for laterality.[13]

2.2.6.1 Test Procedure – Finger and Thumb Opposition Test

Test position – standing.

Stand with feet or heels together.

Bend the elbow of one arm so that the forearm and hand are held out in front at a 45° angle with the palm of the hand facing the child. The opposite arm should hang loosely by the side.

Bend the thumb and first finger to form a circle (Figure 2.6). (It is advisable for the tester to demonstrate the position required.)

Open and close the circle between the thumb and forefinger using the tip of the thumb and finger five times.

Repeat the movement five times using the thumb and the second (middle) finger. Continue the sequence with the remaining two fingers.

Return the arm to a resting position alongside the body.

Repeat the whole test sequence using the other hand.

2.2.6.2 Observations

- Do the fingers of the opposite hand also move, that is, do they 'mirror' the movements of the active hand? If so, how much, and with which fingers?
- Is the child able to make the sequential movements?
- Does the child have difficulty with one or several fingers? Which ones?
- Does the thumb lose the ability to make the tip of the finger 'hit' the tip of the thumb?

2.2.6.3 Scoring

0. No abnormality detected.
1. Slight mirroring in the fingers of the opposite hand, and/or control of balance is slightly impaired.
2. More noticeable mirroring of the fingers in the opposite hand, clarity of movement in one finger may be poor.

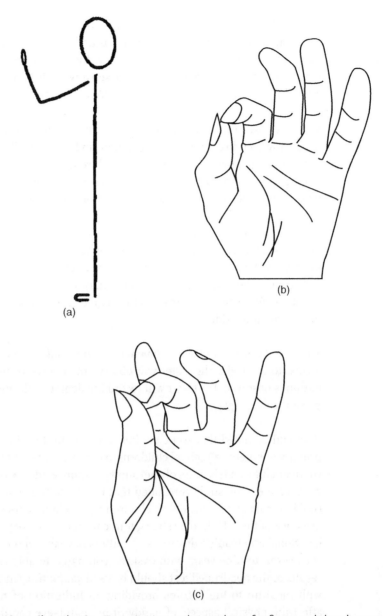

Figure 2.6a, 2.6b and 2.6c   Test position and procedures for finger and thumb opposition test

3. Definite mirroring of the fingers in the opposite hand. Ability to juxtapose the fingertip and the tip of the thumb is lost.
4. The child was unable to carry out the task.

▶ 2.3   TESTS FOR PRIMITIVE REFLEXES

2.3.1   ASYMMETRICAL TONIC NECK REFLEX (ATNR)

There are a variety of tests available to test for the continued presence of the ATNR. In young babies, the reflex is assessed in the supine position (lying on the back) with the tester gently rotating the head to each side and observing whether there is extension in the limbs on the side to which the head is turned and flexion in the limbs on the occipital (back of the head) side.

The supine test is suitable for use with very young children or individuals with physical handicap. However, as children develop muscle tone, the ATNR can be 'masked' by alteration in muscle tension during testing and for this reason the supine test is not included in the screening tests for this age group. More sensitive tests for eliciting the ATNR in older children and adults include the quadruped test (Ayres)[14] and the Hoff–Schilder Test.[15]

When assessed under *clinical* conditions, a trained therapist would normally rotate the child's head. However, to comply with regulations in the United Kingdom which discourage teachers from making physical contact with children, and to enable professionals who have not undergone specific training in the assessment of primitive reflexes to assess the selected reflexes, these tests have been adapted to avoid the tester having physical contact with the child.

In the quadruped test, the child is instructed to go on to hands and knees in a 'table' position (all fours, Figure 2.7) with the back of the head held level with the spine, and to gently turn the head as far as possible to one side. If the ATNR is present, as the head is turned, flexion will occur in the *occipital* arm. The reflex may be present on one side only, or differ in strength on either side. The tester observes the degree of flexion in the occipital arm when the head is turned to either side.

The ATNR is scored in the direction to which the head is turned. For example, when the head is turned to the right, the tester will observe the degree of flexion in the *left* occipital arm; if flexion is observed, the tester will record the degree of flexion as evidence of the ATNR being present to the *right*.

It should be noted that some studies have found that the ATNR can be elicited in normal primary (elementary) school children up to the age of eight years on the quadruped test, with younger children (six years of age) showing more evidence of the reflex than children at eight years of age. One study concluded that flexion of the elbow up to 30° on the occipital side could be considered normal in children up to eight years of age,[16] while Silver found the presence of the ATNR to be stronger in children over five years of age with maturational lag, emotional and reading disorders.[17] Others have found the ATNR to be stronger in children aged seven to nine years with dyslexia compared to able readers.[18] Bearing this in mind, results of the quadruped test should be used *qualitatively* in children under eight years of age with medium to high scores providing an indication of neuromotor immaturity likely to affect the physical aspects of handwriting, hand–eye coordination and tasks which involve crossing the midline.

2.3.1.1   Test Procedure – Ayres Test for the ATNR[14]

Test position – hand and knees.

Instruct the child to go on hands and knees into the 'table' or four-point kneeling position (Figure 2.7).

Figure 2.7   Test position for the Ayres test for the ATNR

Instruct the child to slowly rotate his/her head to the right, keeping the head parallel to the shoulder line; when rotated, pause in this position for 5–10 seconds.

Return the head to the midline, pause for 5–10 seconds.

Turn the head to the opposite side; pause for 5–10 seconds.

Return to the midline; pause for 5–10 seconds.

Repeat the sequence four times.

2.3.1.2 Observations

As the child turns his/her head to one side, does the opposite arm or shoulder bend at the elbow, or is there any hip movement outwards on the opposite side?

Score the reflex on the side to which the head is turned.

2.3.1.3 Scoring

0. No movement of the opposite arm, shoulder or hip (**no reflex present**).
1. Slight bending of the opposite arm or movement of the shoulder or hip (**reflex present to 25%**).
2. Definite bending of the opposite arm or movement of the shoulder or hip (**reflex present to 50%**).
3. Marked bending of the opposite arm, with or without shoulder or hip involvement (**reflex present to 75%**).
4. Collapse of the opposite arm as a result of head rotation. There may also be hip involvement (**reflex 100% retained in the arm on the side to which the head is turned**).

2.3.2   THE SYMMETRICAL TONIC NECK REFLEX (STNR)

In the infant, flexion of the head in the quadruped position will elicit bending of the arms and extension of the legs; extension of the head in the quadruped position will elicit extension of the arms and flexion of the legs.

The child is instructed to go on to hands and knees in the 'table' position and to look upwards arching the head (not the back) upwards and backwards. If the reflex is present in extension, as the head is lifted up, the legs bend either pulling the buttocks towards the heels, or the heels towards the buttocks and the arms straighten (Figure 1.3).

The child is then instructed to look down 'as if looking between your knees'. If the reflex is present in flexion as the head is flexed, the arms will bend (Figure 1.4).

2.3.2.1   Test Procedure – Symmetrical Tonic Neck Reflex

Test position – hands and knees.

Instruct the child to go on hands and knees in the four-point kneeling 'table' position (Figure 2.8).

Figure 2.8   Test position for the Symmetrical Tonic Neck Reflex test

The child is instructed to maintain the test position in the arms and the legs and to slowly bend the head down '*as if looking between your knees*'.

Hold the position for five seconds and then slowly move the head upwards '*as if looking at the ceiling*', (keeping the arms straight and the rest of the body still).

Repeat up to six times.

2.3.2.2   Observations

- Note any bending of the arms or raising of the feet as a result of head flexion.
- Note any movement of the trunk backwards as a result of head extension.

2.3.2.3   Scoring

0. No response.
1. Tremor in one or both arms or slight hip movement.
2. Bending of the elbow and/or the hips, or arching of the back.
3. Definite bending of the arms as a result of head flexion.
4. Bending of the arms to the floor in response to flexion of the head, or movement of the bottom back onto the ankles as a result of extension of the head.

2.3.3   TONIC LABYRINTHINE REFLEX (TLR) – ERECT TEST

In the infant, movement of the head through the mid-plane (flexion or extension of the head) will elicit changes in body position and muscle tonus.

When tested in babies and very young children, the test is usually carried out in the supine position. However, as with the ATNR, as children develop postural control and muscle tone, the reflex can be inhibited in positions where there is minimal challenge to balance and posture, for example when lying down, but fail to be inhibited as the challenge to posture and balance increases. The test for the TLR has been adapted to assess the presence of the TLR in the erect (upright) position.

The child is instructed to stand with feet together and arms by the sides with the eyes closed and to slowly tilt the head back 'as if looking towards the ceiling'. If the reflex is present in extension, either during the movement of the head, or when the head is in an extended position, there will be significant increase in muscle tonus throughout the body.

The child is then instructed to slowly bring the head forwards 'as if looking down at your toes'. If the reflex is present in flexion, as the head is flexed, there will be significant increase in flexor muscle tone.

As distribution of muscle tone is involved in the control of both balance and posture, if the reflex is present in either position, head movement can interfere with control of balance.

Traces of the Tonic Labyrinthine Reflex can persist under different postural conditions up to three and a half years of age but should be suppressed from this time.

2.3.3.1   Test procedure – Tonic Labyrinthine Reflex

Test position – standing. Note that it is important for the tester to stand behind or beside the child throughout the test procedure, as movement of the head can result in loss of balance.

Instruct the child to stand with feet together, and arms straight at the sides of the body (Figure 2.9).

Figure 2.9   Test position for the Erect test for the Tonic Labyrinthine Reflex test

Ask the child to slowly tilt the head back into an extended position, 'as if looking up at the ceiling' and then close the eyes. (Stand behind to support in case of loss of balance.) After ten seconds, ask the child to slowly move the head forward, 'as if looking down at your toes', and maintain that position for a further ten seconds. Repeat the sequence 5–6 times.

2.3.3.2   Observations

- Note any loss of balance or alteration of balance which results from movement of the head forwards or backwards.
- Observe any compensatory changes in muscle tone at the back of the knees, or gripping with the toes which occurs when the head is moved through the mid-plane.

- Ask the child how he/she feels immediately after testing, and note any comments about feelings of dizziness or nausea during the testing – both of which suggest faulty vestibular/ proprioceptive interaction and/or the residual presence of the tonic labyrinthine reflex.

2.3.3.3 Scoring

0. No response.
1. Slight alteration of balance and muscle tone as a result of change in head position.
2. Impairment of balance during test and/or alteration of muscle tone.
3. Near loss of balance and/or alteration of muscle tone and/or disorientation as a result of test procedure.
4. Loss of balance and/or marked adjustment in muscle tone in an attempt to stabilize balance. This may be accompanied by dizziness or disorientation.

▶ 2.4 TESTS FOR VISUAL PERCEPTION AND VISUAL-MOTOR INTEGRATION

The following two tests have been selected from tests for visual perception and visual-motor maturity originally developed by AE Tansley.[19]

The Tansley Standard Figures are based on drawing tests originally devised by Gesell for the assessment of fine motor abilities and visual-perceptual motor skills. There is a developmental age at which a child should be able to copy each of the shapes. Discrepancy between a child's ability to produce an age-appropriate drawing and chronological age provides one indication of immaturity in visual-perceptual motor skills.

(a) **Visual perception**

Visual perception describes the brain's ability to interpret and make sense of visual images seen with the eyes, enabling the brain to interpret correctly what is seen. This involves much more than simply adequate eyesight and is the product of multi-sensory and motor experience combined with vision and other information derived from other sensory systems together with operations in space.

(b) **Visual-motor integration (VMI)**

Visual-motor integration refers to the ability to coordinate motor movement with a visual stimulus. The child with a difficulty in this area has problems coordinating what he/she sees with an appropriate motor response required in fine motor skills, as, for example, in copying, writing and drawing. VMI involves visual perception combined with motor coordination to achieve accurate reproduction of the model. Difficulties with visual-motor integration may be seen in:

- Control of the pencil affecting the quality of the line.
- Poor closure of shapes at the corners.
- Inability to cross the midline with the horizontal and diagonal lines seen on the Union Jack shape.
- Continued difficulty with crossing the midline with diagonal lines.

(c) **Spatial difficulties**

Spatial difficulties may be evident in the size, orientation and layout of figures on the page. Mild spatial problems can be seen in irregularity of the size of shapes or in a row of shapes sloping in one direction.

Test position – sitting.

At the outset the child is asked to sit at a bare table or desk, and is presented with a piece of unlined A4 paper and a sharpened pencil.

- The child is then given the Figure 2.10 from which to copy.

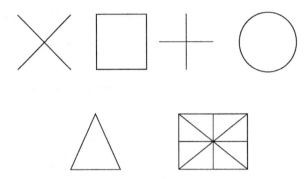

Figure 2.10   Pencil and paper tests based on the Tansley standard visual figures test

- The child is asked to draw the circle in a clockwise direction. The tester should demonstrate using a finger the direction in which the circle should be formed.
- (From five years of age) The child is asked to draw a second circle, this time forming the shape in an anti-clockwise direction. The tester should demonstrate using a finger the direction in which the second circle should be formed.

A child should be able to copy a circle with some degree of accuracy in a clockwise direction by three years of age. A right-handed child should be able to draw a circle using an anti-clockwise motion from five years of age.

The ability to draw a circle in either direction is necessary to form letter shapes correctly and is, therefore, a physical precursor to writing.

- The child is then given the Figure 2.11 from which to copy.
- The child is asked to copy the vertical line, horizontal line and diagonal line.

Ask the child to copy only the shapes below that are commensurate with the chronological age of the child.

1. Copy the + sign   from $3^{1}/_{2}$ years
2. Copy the square   from 4 years
3. Copy the X   from $4^{1}/_{2}$ years
4. Copy the triangle   from 6 years
5. Copy the Union Jack shape   from $6^{1}/_{2}$ years of age)[†]

[†] If the Union Jack figure is used with children under five years of age, they will tend to use horizontal lines which do not cross the midline; from 5 to 6 years of age some of the diagonal lines will cross the vertical midline; children with learning disabilities tend to draw lines from the centre outwards, indicating continued difficulties with crossing the midline.

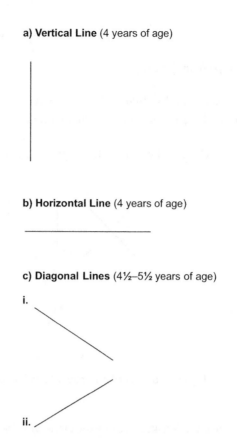

a) Vertical Line (4 years of age)

b) Horizontal Line (4 years of age)

c) Diagonal Lines (4½–5½ years of age)

i.

ii.

Figure 2.11 Pencil and paper tests based on lines

6. On a separate sheet of paper ask the child to copy:
   a) vertical line   from 4 years
   b) horizontal line   from 4 years
   c) diagonal line   from $4^{1}/_{2}$ to $5^{1}/_{2}$ years

2.4.1.1 Observations (Visual Figures)

- Does the child produce a recognisable age-appropriate drawing?
- Does the child use an appropriate pencil grip?
- Does the child show dissatisfaction with his or her work and/or ask for an eraser?
- Does the child find it very difficult to complete?
- Is there marked deviation/lean to one side in the child's drawing of the vertical line?
- Note any alteration of posture or position of the paper when carrying out these tasks.

2.4.1.2 Scoring (Visual Figures)

0. Completed all the drawings up to his/her chronological age.
1. There is a definite tremor evident on all the drawings, that is, visual-motor integration difficulties, and/or immature pencil grip.
2. Can only complete up to drawing three below his/her age-related drawing.
3. Can only complete the first two drawings.
4. The drawings, with the possible exception of the circles, are not exact copies of the shapes.

2.4.1.3   Observations (Lines)

- Vertical line – does the line lean markedly in one direction? Which direction?
- Vertical and horizontal lines – is the line reasonably straight or is there marked 'wobble' in control of the pencil?
- Does the child form the line with one movement or does he/she use a series of small approximation strokes?
- Diagonal lines – does the child draw a diagonal? Is he/she able to copy the diagonal line from left (top) to right (bottom) and from right (top) to left (bottom)? (from $5^{1}/_{2}+$ years).

2.4.1.4   Scoring (Lines)

The scoring system is not applied to the drawing of vertical, horizontal or diagonal lines. The test is simply used for observation purposes.

Record any of the above observations on the observation sheet.

2.4.2   ADDITIONAL MEASURES

2.4.2.1   Draw a Person Test

Children's drawings provide a measure of developmental progress and delay. In 1921 Burt[20] stated that developmental progress and evidence of delay could be observed in children's drawings and, in 1926, Goodenough[21] published findings using the 'Draw a Man Test', which showed that children's drawings are linked to intelligence. Goodenough's test was refined by Harris in 1963[22] and since that time the scoring system in The Goodenough–Harris Drawing Test has been shown to correlate with intelligence tests such as the Wechsler and Binet scales.

While many factors (visual-motor integration difficulties for example) can contribute to difficulties with the mechanical aspects of drawing, the Draw a Person Test provides *one* measure of nonverbal cognitive performance. A number of scoring systems are available to assess a child's drawing of the human figure. Irrespective of which scoring system is used, a child's drawing of the human figure can provide useful additional information concerning:

- Discrepancy between mental age compared to chronological age or percentile score on the test as *one* measure of nonverbal performance.
- A child's awareness of his/her body image.
- Evidence of neuromotor factors affecting nonverbal performance.

Findings from studies using the INPP Developmental Exercise Programme for use in Schools have shown consistent improvement in drawing skills, including the Draw a Person Test, following intervention.[23] Improvements in nonverbal performance are important because up to 90% of effective communication is based on the nonverbal aspects of language. Nonverbal skills are also linked to visuospatial skills which support many other aspects of learning.

Used in this context, the Draw a Person Test can provide a useful additional measure both for identification of signs of immaturity in nonverbal performance and as an objective measurement of change following intervention.

2.4.2.2 Reading Age or National Curriculum Assessment for Reading, Writing and Maths (from Five Years of Age)

Reading age or national curriculum assessment for reading, writing and maths provide additional objective measures of a child's performance on verbal, motor and numerical tasks.

These assessments can either be repeated after intervention or extracted from individual national curriculum records before and after intervention to evaluate whether improvements in neuromotor performance cross over into educational performance.

Date	1st assessment	2nd assessment

Name
Code number
Age of Child

1. Neuromotor tests

	1st assessment	2nd assessment
Romberg Test (eyes open)	0 1 2 3 4	0 1 2 3 4
Romberg Test (eyes closed)	0 1 2 3 4	0 1 2 3 4
One leg stand (right leg)	0 1 2 3 4	0 1 2 3 4
One leg stand (left leg)	0 1 2 3 4	0 1 2 3 4
Creeping on hands and knees	0 1 2 3 4	0 1 2 3 4
Crossing the midline (1)	0 1 2 3 4	0 1 2 3 4
Crossing the midline (2)	0 1 2 3 4	0 1 2 3 4
Finger and thumb opposition (right hand)	0 1 2 3 4	0 1 2 3 4
Finger and thumb opposition (left hand)	0 1 2 3 4	0 1 2 3 4
Asymmetrical Tonic Neck Reflex (right)	0 1 2 3 4	0 1 2 3 4
Asymmetrical Tonic Neck Reflex (left)	0 1 2 3 4	0 1 2 3 4
Symmetrical Tonic Neck Reflex (flexion)	0 1 2 3 4	0 1 2 3 4
Symmetrical Tonic Neck Reflex (extension)	0 1 2 3 4	0 1 2 3 4
Tonic Labyrinthine Reflex (flexion)	0 1 2 3 4	0 1 2 3 4
Tonic Labyrinthine Reflex (extension)	0 1 2 3 4	0 1 2 3 4
Total – neuromotor tests	/60	/60

2. Visual-perceptual tests

	1st assessment	2nd assessment
Tansley Standard Figures – circle	0 1 2 3 4	0 1 2 3 4
Tansley Standard Figures – cross	0 1 2 3 4	0 1 2 3 4
Tansley Standard Figures – square	0 1 2 3 4	0 1 2 3 4
Tansley Standard Figures – X	0 1 2 3 4	0 1 2 3 4
Tansley Standard Figures – triangle	0 1 2 3 4	0 1 2 3 4
Tansley Standard Figures – Union Jack	0 1 2 3 4	0 1 2 3 4
Total – visual-perceptual tests	/24	/24

Additional assessments
Draw a person (mental age)
Reading age (or National Curriculum
   Assessments for Reading, Writing
   and Maths)
Spelling

▶ 2.6 OBSERVATION SHEETS

Date   1st assessment   2nd assessment

Name
Code Number
Age of Child

1. Neuromotor tests
Romberg Test (eyes open)
Romberg Test (eyes closed)
One Leg Stand (right leg)
One Leg Stand (left leg)
Creeping on hands and knees
Crossing the midline 1
Crossing the midline 2
Finger and thumb opposition (right
    hand)
Finger and thumb opposition (left
    hand)
Asymmetrical Tonic Neck Reflex
    (right)
Asymmetrical Tonic Neck Reflex (left)
Symmetrical Tonic Neck Reflex
    (flexion)
Symmetrical Tonic Neck Reflex
    (extension)
Tonic Labyrinthine Reflex (flexion)
Tonic Labyrinthine Reflex (extension)

2. Visual-perceptual tests
Tansley Standard Figures – circle
Tansley Standard Figures – cross
Tansley Standard Figures – square
Tansley Standard Figures – X
Tansley Standard Figures – triangle
Tansley Standard Figures – Union Jack
Vertical line (4 years)
Horizontal line (4 years)
Diagonal line ($4^1/_2$–5 years)

Additional assessments:
Draw a person (mental age)
Reading age (or National Curriculum
    Assessments for Reading, Writing
    and Maths)
Spelling

▶ 2.7 INTERPRETING THE SCORES

The final scores have been divided into different sections to identify whether signs of immaturity are more prevalent in one or several areas of functioning.

Scores are interpreted in five categories:

1. **No abnormality detected (NAD)**
2. **Low score**   <25%
3. **Medium score**   25–50%
4. **High score**   50–75%
5. **Very high score**   75–100%

2.7.1 TESTS FOR GROSS MUSCLE COORDINATION, BALANCE AND REFLEXES

1. **NAD**   No action required.
2. **Low score**   No action required but child may benefit from participating in the INPP developmental exercise programme.
3. **Medium score**   INPP developmental exercise programme recommended.
4. **High score**   INPP developmental exercise programme recommended but additional referral for more detailed investigations may also be indicated. Children in this group may also benefit from an *individual* reflex integration programme devised by an INPP practitioner following a full neuro-developmental assessment.
5. **Very high score**   Referral through family doctor for further professional assessment. Possible diagnosis and professional intervention or support indicated.

2.7.2 TESTS FOR VISUAL PERCEPTION AND VISUAL-MOTOR INTEGRATION

If scores in *both* this section *and* the section for gross muscle coordination, balance and reflexes range from medium to high, improvements will often be seen in visual perception and visual-motor integration as neuromotor skills mature following use of the INPP Developmental Movement Programme.

If scores for visual perception and visual-motor integration fall anywhere in the low to very high range, but scores for gross muscle coordination, balance and reflexes fall within the normal range, referral to an optometrist for a full vision test is recommended. If vision is normal when tested at far and near distance, but problems are still evident on tests for visual perception, it *might* indicate a specific oculomotor dysfunction. Referral to an orthoptist might be indicated.

▶ REFERENCES

[1] De Quiros, JB and Schrager, O (1979) *Neuropsychological fundamentals in learning disabilities.* Academic Therapy Publications, Novato, CA.
[2] Schrager, O (2000) Balance control, age and language development. Paper presented at The European Conference of Neuro-Developmental Delay in Children with Specific Learning Difficulties, Chester, UK. March (2000)

[3] Schrager, O (1994/1999) Tonic postural reactions and language development. Towards a neuro-psychological model of dysphasic disorders. Doctoral dissertation. PhD program in 'Cognition and its Disorders'. Department of Basic Psychology. School of Psychology. Autonomous University of Madrid/UAM, Madrid, Spain.

[4] Drillien, CM and Drummond, MB (1977) *Neurodevelopmental problems in early childhood.* Blackwell Publishing Ltd, Oxford.

[5] Ayres, AJ (1970) *Sensory integration and the child.* Western Psychological Services, Los Angeles, CA.

[6] Portwood, M (2003) *Developmental dyspraxia: Identification and intervention.* David Fulton Publishers, London.

[7] Kranowitz, CS (2005) *The out of sync child.* Perigree Books, New York.

[8] Haywood, K and Gretchell, N (2008) *Life span development.* Human Kinetics, Champaign, IL.

[9] Kuhlman, F (1939) *Tests of mental development.* Educational Test Bureau. Minneapolis, MN.

[10] Touwen, BCL (1970) *Examination of the child with minor neurological dysfunction.* William Heinemann Medical Books, London.

[11] Grant, WW, Boelshce, AN and Zin, D (1973) Developmental patterns of two motor functions. *Dev. Med. Child Neurolog.*, **15**: 171–177.

[12] Satz, P, Taylor, HG, Friel, J and Fletcher, JM (1978) Some developmental and predictive precursors of reading disabilities. A six year follow-up. In: Benton, AL and Pearl, D (eds), *Dyslexia. An appraisal of current knowledge.* Oxford University Press, New York.

[13] Kohen-Raz, R (1996) *Learning disabilities and postural control.* Freund Publishing House Ltd, London

[14] Ayres, AJ (1978) *Sensory integration and learning disorders.* Western Psychological Services, Los Angeles, CA.

[15] Hoff, H and Schilder, P (1927) *Die Lagereflexe des Menschen. Klinische Untersuchungen über Haltungs-und Stellreflexe und verwandte Phänomene.* Julius Springer, Vienna, Austria.

[16] Parmentier, CL (1975) The asymmetrical tonic neck reflex in normal first and third grade children. *The American Journal of Occupational Therapy,* **29**(8): 463–468.

[17] Silver, AA (1952) Postural and righting responses in children. *J. Pediatr.,* **41**: 493–498.

[18] McPhillips, M and Jordan Black, JA (2007) Primary reflex persistence in children with reading difficulties (dyslexia): A cross-sectional study. *Neuropsychologia,* **45**: 748–754.

[19] Tansley, AE (1967) *Reading and remedial reading.* Routledge and Kegan Paul Ltd, London.

[20] Burt, C (1921) *Mental and scholastic tests.* PS King & Son, London.

[21] Goodenough, F (1926) *Measurement of intelligence by drawings.* Yonkers-on-Hudson, World Book Co., New York.

[22] Harris, DB (1963) *Children's drawings as measures of intellectual maturity.* Harcourt, Brace & World, Inc., New York.

[23] Goddard Blythe, SA (2005) Releasing educational potential through movement. A summary of individual studies using The INPP Test Battery and Developmental Exercise Programme for use in Schools with Children with Special Needs. *Child Care in Practice,* **11**(4): 415–432.

3

Developmental Screening Tests for Use with Children from 7 Years of Age

▶ **3.1   GENERAL INSTRUCTIONS**

All tests have been adapted to comply with regulations (in the United Kingdom) that teachers should avoid physical contact with children in their care.

Testing should be carried out with the child wearing loose clothing and in bare feet.

To ensure that the child has understood verbal instructions correctly, the tester should also demonstrate the beginning of each test procedure.

Additional notes of observations made during tests should be recorded on the separate observation sheets provided and attached to the score sheet.

Please note that some tests are developmentally appropriate from eight years of age. Omit tests where it states that the developmental norm for the test is older than the age of the child being assessed, unless it states that the test may be used for *qualitative* purposes at a younger age.

Qualitative observations enable the tester to observe the quality of performance. This can be re-assessed at a later date or following intervention to observe whether there has been significant change in the quality of performance over time.

Video examples of test positions, observations and scoring may be found at www.accessnmr. inpp.org.uk. Registration on this site will enable one month's free access to supporting material for testing, exercises and application of the programme in schools.

3.1.1   SCORING

All tests are scored using a 5-point rating scale:

0. no abnormality detected (NAD)
1. 25% dysfunction
2. 50% dysfunction
3. 75% dysfunction
4. 100% dysfunction

Assessing Neuromotor Readiness for Learning: The INPP Developmental Screening Test and School Intervention Programme, First Edition. Sally Goddard Blythe.
© 2012 John Wiley & Sons, Ltd. Published 2012 by John Wiley & Sons, Ltd.

Tests to assess gross muscle coordination and balance:

1. The Tandem Walk
2. Walking on the outsides of the feet (the Fog test)

Tests for aberrant reflexes:

1. The Asymmetrical Tonic Neck Reflex (ATNR)
   a) The Quadruped test (Ayres)
   b) The Erect test (Adapted from Hoff–Schilder)[1]
2. The Symmetrical Tonic Neck Reflex (STNR)
3. The Tonic Labyrinthine Reflex (TLR)

Tests to assess oculomotor functioning:

1. Test for visual tracking and control of saccadic eye movements (Valett)
2. Test for visual integration (Valett)

Tests for visual-speech recognition of sounds:

1. Individual sounds
2. Sound blends
3. Syllables
4. Synthesis

Tests for visual perception and visual-motor integration:

1. The Tansley Standard Figures
2. Figures based upon the Bender Visual Motor Gestalt Test

▶ 3.2   TESTS FOR GROSS MUSCLE COORDINATION AND BALANCE

3.2.1   TANDEM WALK

A test used primarily to assess balance, gait and signs of possible cerebellar involvement.

Children with neurological immaturity will tend to show signs of clumsiness, accessory movements and loss of control on this test. The Tandem Walk can also reveal evidence of difficulty with control of balance and postural adjustment at the midline and proprioception. Evidence of poor proprioceptive awareness may be observed in the placement of the feet when carrying out this test.

Both the Tandem Walk and walking on the outsides of the feet (Fog Walk) are carried out forwards and backwards. When going forwards, vision acts as the leading sense in controlling balance and coordination; when going backwards, balance and proprioception taking over the leading roles. If a child's performance is *consistently and significantly* better on *both* tests in one direction only, it might indicate:

(a) Forwards better than backwards – vision is being used to compensate for difficulties with balance and/or proprioception.
(b) Backwards better than forwards – vision is not well calibrated with balance and proprioception.

3.2.1.1 Test Procedure – The Tandem Walk

Test position – standing; eyes open.

(a) Forwards: Instruct the child to walk *slowly* in a straight line with the heel of the leading foot making contact with the toes of the trailing foot each time the leading foot is placed on the ground (Figure 3.1).

Figure 3.1   Test position for the tandem walk

(b) Backwards: Instruct the child to walk *slowly* in a straight line with the toe of the leading foot making contact with heel of the trailing foot then the leading foot is placed on the ground.

3.2.1.2 Observations

General: Note any problems with balance, coordination, and position of the limbs.

- Observe control of balance. Is there marked difficulty in maintaining balance?
- Does the child need to hold his/her arms out in a primary balance position or use excessive arm movements in order to complete the test? (Indicative of difficulty with maintaining balance over a narrow base of support.)
- Check accuracy of foot placement (proprioceptive awareness).
- Overall degree of difficulty/concentration used to carry out the task.
- Is there 'overflow' of movement (for example facial, mouth or tongue involvement)?

3.2.1.3   Scoring

0. No abnormality detected.
1. Minimal problems noted with the following: balance or foot placement; tendency to fixate visually on one point; slight facial involvement; tendency to look down; slight hand or arm involvement.
2. Increase in any or several of the above observations; use of 'primary balance' position; some difficulty in controlling balance at the midline.
3. Near loss of balance; arms extended; sway in arms and/or body; inaccuracy in foot placement.
4. Loss of balance with or without marked increase in any of the above observations.

Note any difference in performance between going forwards and backwards; score separately forwards and backwards using the above criteria.

3.2.2   WALKING ON THE OUTSIDES OF THE FEET (FOG TEST[2])

A test primarily used in medicine to elicit vertical synkinesia.[*]

The child is instructed to walk slowly in a straight line on the outsides of the feet keeping the arms to the sides.

Going on to the outsides of the feet can elicit abnormal posturing of the upper extremities. Associated movements should disappear by 10–13 years of age, but the test may be used *qualitatively* with younger children from $7^1/_2$ years of age.[3]

Associated movements are defined as movements which accompany a motor function, are not involved in the specific motor function and are not necessary to its performance. The persistence of associated movements is a sign supporting other evidence of immaturity in the brain or of poor development of discriminatory, selective motor activity.[2]

3.2.2.1   Test Procedure – The Fog Walk

Test position – standing; eyes open.

(a) Forwards: Instruct the child to walk *slowly* in a straight line on the outsides of the feet for a distance of approximately four metres (Figure 3.2).
(b) Backwards: After completing the distance forwards, instruct the child to stop, put the feet together and stand still; then to repeat the procedure going backwards.

3.2.2.2   Observations

Note any:

- Difficulty staying on the outside of the feet.
- Alteration in posture.
- Coordination.

---

[*] Synkinesia – the performing of an unintended movement when making a voluntary one.

Figure 3.2   Test position for the Fog walk

- Position of the hands and arms.
- Movements of the mouth.

Note any difference in performance between going forwards and backwards; score separately forwards and backwards using the above criteria.

3.2.2.3   Scoring

0. No abnormality detected.
1. Slight involuntary hand involvement on one side.
2. Hand involvement on both sides and/or slight postural alteration, or not fully on the outsides of the feet and/or facial involvement.
3. Simian posture or stiff gait with homolateral movements or marked hemiplegia.
4. Marked simian posture, unable to move or complete the task.

▶ 3.3   TESTS FOR ABERRANT PRIMITIVE REFLEXES

Further information regarding the assessment of primitive reflexes can be found elsewhere.[4]

3.3.1   THE ASYMMETRICAL TONIC NECK REFLEX (ATNR)

There are a variety of tests available to test for the continued presence of the ATNR. In young babies, the reflex is tested in the supine position (lying on the back) with the tester gently rotating the head to each side and observing whether there is extension in the limbs on the side to which the head is turned and flexion in the limbs on the occipital (back of the head) side.

The supine test is useful with very young children or individuals with physical handicap. However, as children develop muscle tone, the ATNR can be 'masked' by alteration of muscle tension during testing, and for this reason the supine test is not included in the screening tests for this age group. More sensitive tests for eliciting the ATNR in older children and adults include the quadruped test (Ayres)[5] and the adapted Hoff–Schilder test.[1]

If assessed under clinical conditions, a trained therapist would normally turn the child's head. However, in order to comply with regulations in the United Kingdom which prevent teachers from making physical contact with children, and to enable professionals who have not undergone specific training in the assessment of primitive reflexes to carry out selected reflex tests, these tests have been adapted to avoid the tester making physical contact with the child.

In the quadruped test, the child is instructed to go on to hands and knees in a 'table' position (all fours) (Figure 3.1) with the back of the head held level with the spine, and to gently turn the head as far as possible to one side. If the ATNR is present, as the head is turned flexion will occur in the arm on the *opposite* side. The reflex may be present on one side only, or differ in strength on either side. The tester records the degree of flexion in the occipital arm when the head is turned to either side.

The reflex is scored on the side to which the head is turned. That is, when the head is turned to the right, the tester observes the degree of flexion in the *left* (occipital) arm. If flexion in the left arm occurs when the head is turned to the right, the ATNR is scored as being present to the *right*.

It should be noted that some studies have found that the ATNR can be elicited in normal primary (elementary) school children up to the age of eight years on the quadruped test, with younger children (six years of age) showing more evidence of the reflex than children at eight years of age. One study concluded that flexion of the elbow up to 30° on the occipital side could be considered normal in children up to eight years of age,[6] while Silver found the presence of the ATNR to be stronger in children over five years of age with maturational lag, emotional and reading disorders[7] and others have found the ATNR to be stronger in children aged 7–9 years with dyslexia compared to able readers.[8] Bearing this in mind, results of the quadruped test should be used *qualitatively* in children under eight years of age with medium to high scores providing an indication of neuromotor immaturity.

The adapted Hoff–Schilder Arm Extension test assesses the presence of the ATNR in the erect position. The child is instructed to stand with feet together, arms held out to the front of the body, wrists flexed and eyes closed. He/she is then asked to slowly turn the head to one side, but to keep the arms in their starting position; that is, when the head turns, the arms should remain still. If the ATNR is present, when the head turns to one side, one or both arms will follow the direction of the head movement. The Arm Extension test is considered to be reliable with children from six years of age.[5]

3.3.1.1 Test Procedure –The Quadruped (Ayres)[5] Test for the ATNR

Test position – hand and knees; eyes open.

Instruct the child to go on hands and knees into the 'table' or four-point kneeling position (Figure 3.3).

Figure 3.3   Test position for the quadruped test for the ATNR

Instruct the child to slowly rotate his/her head to the right, keeping the back of the head in line with the spine and ensuring the head rotation remains parallel to the shoulder line. Pause in this position for 5–10 seconds.

Return the head to the midline.

Slowly rotate the head to the left. Pause for 5–10 seconds.

Return the head to the midline.

Repeat the sequence up to four times.

3.3.1.2   Observations (Ayres Test)

As the child turns his/her head to one side, does the opposite arm or shoulder bend at the elbow, or is there any hip movement outwards on the opposite side? The reflex is scored in *the same direction as the head movement*. That is, if the head is turned to the right and the left arm flexes, the ATNR will be scored to the right according to the degree of flexion present in the occipital limb.

3.3.1.3   Scoring (Ayres Test)

0. No movement of the opposite arm, shoulder or hip (**no reflex present**).
1. Slight bending of the opposite arm (30°) or movement of the shoulder or hip (**reflex present to 25%**).
2. Definite bending of the opposite arm (45°) or movement of the shoulder or hip (**reflex present to 50%**).
3. Marked bending of the opposite arm (>45°), with or without shoulder or hip involvement (**reflex present to 75%**).
4. Collapse of the opposite arm as a result of head rotation. There may also be hip involvement (**reflex 100% retained in the arm on the side to which the head is turned**).

3.3.1.4   Test Procedure – The Erect Adapted (Hoff–Schilder)[1] Test for the ATNR

Test position – standing.

Instruct the child to stand, feet together, with the arms held out straight in front, at shoulder width and shoulder height, but with the hands relaxed at the wrists† (Figure 3.4). The tester should stand behind the child.

---

† The original Hoff–Schilder Test has the hands extended.

It is important to stand behind the child during this test, as some children with a retained ATNR lose their balance when the head is turned or when the eyes are closed.

Figure 3.4   Test position for the Hoff–Schilder Test for the ATNR

When this position is established, and the verbal instructions have been completed, the eyes should then be *closed*.

Instruct the child to:

'Slowly turn your head to one side (through to 90 degrees), but keep your arms still if you can. This means that your arms remain in the same position, and only your head moves; close your eyes'.

The head should rotate slowly until the chin is parallel with the shoulder. When the head is fully rotated to one side instruct the child to:

pause for 5–10 seconds;
return the head to the midline;
pause for 5–10 seconds;
rotate the head to the other side;
pause for 5–10 seconds.

Repeat the procedure up to four times.

3.3.1.5   Observations (Hoff–Schilder Test)

Note any movement of the arm and hand on the side to which the head is turned; that is, do one or both arms move in the same direction with the head?

3.3.1.6   Scoring (Hoff–Schilder Test)

0. No response.
1. Slight movement of the arms in the same direction as the head movement.
2. Movement of the arms together with the head by 45°.
3. Arm movement by as much as 60°.
4. 90° rotation of the arms and/or loss of balance as a result of head rotation.

In the infant, flexion of the head in the quadruped position will elicit bending of the arms and extension of the legs; extension of the head in the quadruped position will elicit extension of the arms and flexion of the legs.

The child is instructed to go on to hands and knees in the 'table' position and to look upwards arching the head (not the back) upwards and backwards. If the reflex is present in extension, as the head is lifted up, the legs bend either pulling the buttocks towards the heels, or the heels towards the buttocks and the arms straighten (seen in the infant in Figure 1.3).

The child is then instructed to look down 'as if looking between your knees'. If the reflex is present in flexion as the head is flexed, the arms will bend (seen in the infant in Figure 1.4).

3.3.2.1   Test Procedure – Symmetrical Tonic Neck Reflex

Test position – hands and knees; eyes open.

Instruct the child to go on to hands and knees in the four-point kneeling 'table' position (Figure 3.5).

Figure 3.5   Test position for the STNR

The child is instructed to maintain the test position but to slowly bend the head down *'as if looking between your knees'*. Hold the position for five seconds.

Slowly move the head upwards *'as if looking towards the ceiling keeping your arms straight and the rest of your body still'*.

Repeat the sequence up to six times.

3.3.2.2   Observations

Note any bending of the arms or raising of the feet as a result of head flexion, or movement of the trunk as a result of head extension.

3.3.2.3   Scoring

0. No response.
1. Tremor in one or both arms or slight hip movement.
2. Slight movement of the elbow and/or the hips in response to flexion of the head, or arching of the back.
3. Definite flexion in the arms as a result of head flexion.

4. Flexion of the arms so that the head is nearly touching the floor in response to flexion of the head, or movement of the bottom back onto the ankles in response to extension of the head.

3.3.3   THE TONIC LABYRINTHINE REFLEX (TLR)

In the infant movement of the head through the mid-plane (flexion or extension of the head) will elicit changes in body position and muscle tonus.

When tested in babies and very young children, the test is usually carried out in the supine position. However, as with the ATNR, as children develop postural control and muscle tone, the reflex can be inhibited in positions where there is minimal challenge to balance and posture, for example, when lying down, but fail to be inhibited as the challenge to posture and balance increases. The test for the TLR has been adapted to assess the presence of the TLR in the erect (upright) position.

The child is instructed to stand with feet together and arms by the sides with the eyes closed and to slowly tilt the head back '*as if looking towards the ceiling*'. If the reflex is present in extension, either during the movement of the head, or when the head is in an extended position there will be significant increase in muscle tonus throughout the body.

The child is then instructed to slowly bring the head forwards, keeping the eyes closed, '*as if looking down at your toes*'. If the reflex is present in flexion, as the head is flexed, there will be significant increase in flexor muscle tone.

As distribution of muscle tone is involved in the control of both balance and posture, if the reflex is present in either position, head movement may destabilise balance.

3.3.3.1   Test Procedure – The Erect Test for the TLR

Test position – standing.

Instruct the child to stand with feet together, and arms straight at the sides of the body (Figure 3.6).

Figure 3.6   Test position for the erect test for the TLR

Instruct the child to slowly tilt the head back into an extended position, '*as if looking up at the ceiling*' and then *close the eyes*. (Stand behind to support in case of loss of balance.) After 10 seconds, instruct the child to slowly move the head forwards, '*as if looking down at your toes*'. Maintain head in flexed position for a further 10 seconds.

Repeat the sequence up to four times.

3.3.3.2 Observations

- Note any loss of balance or alteration of balance which results from movement of the head forwards or backwards.
- Observe any compensatory changes in muscle tone at the back of the knees, or gripping with the toes which occurs when the head is moved.
- Ask the child how he/she feels immediately after testing, and note any comments about feelings of dizziness or nausea during the testing – both of which suggest faulty vestibular/proprioceptive interaction and/or the residual presence of the tonic labyrinthine reflex.

3.3.3.3 Scoring

0. No response.
1. Slight destabilisation of balance as a result of head movement/change of position.
2. Impairment of balance during test and/or alteration of muscle tone in the legs.
3. Near loss of balance and/or alteration of muscle tone in the legs and/or disorientation as a result of test procedure.
4. Loss of balance and/or marked adjustment in muscle tone in attempt to stabilise balance. This may be accompanied by dizziness or disorientation.

▶ 3.4 TESTS FOR OCULOMOTOR FUNCTIONING

Reading, or the ability to follow a line of print and derive meaning from the pattern of symbols on the page, requires the development of a complex series of eye movements beginning with the ability to find a visual 'fixation' point on the page.

Fixation depends on the ability of the two eyes to converge on the fixation point. Convergence is the process by which the two separate images seen by each eye independently 'fuse' into a single clear image.

The two eyes then make a small sweeping movement to another fixation point further along the page. This movement is called a 'saccade'. The purpose of saccades is to move the eyes as quickly as possible to the next position, so the point of interest is centred on the fovea. The fovea is the area of the eye where focus is at its sharpest.

After each saccade, the eyes pause (fixate) and then may make a small regressive movement, to check or re-check any relevant information that may have been missed in the previous saccade. The size of saccades is constantly adjusted according to the size of the text, words and number of words on a line. At the end of each line, the eyes must make a large regressive movement to start reading at the beginning of the next line.

Any problems with visual fixation, convergence or control of saccades can affect fluency, accuracy and comprehension when reading. The following test, based on one originally developed by Valett (1980),[9] can help to identify problems with any one or combination of the series of eye movements needed to support reading.

3.4.1   TEST FOR FIXATION, CONVERGENCE AND CONTROL OF SACCADES (VALETT[9])

3.4.1.1   Test Procedure

Test position – standing.

Instruct the child to say every alternate symbol aloud from the lines shown. This procedure should be carried out as quickly as possible without finger pointing. Scoring will be determined by accuracy.

DS 7LY N 2BTEK P 83

1 C OP MW9

4U JQ6HX V F5Z A

M WS3L

3.4.2   TEST FOR VISUAL INTEGRATION

In order to focus visual attention at near point it is necessary to be able to ignore both background and peripheral visual information. This depends on being able to maintain near-point convergence. Children with poorly developed near-point convergence tend either to get 'lost' in the pattern, or the eyes are attracted to the periphery (visual stimulus bound effect) and are unable to count the number of symbols in the test below without using a finger to point to individual shapes or going back to check and re-check that they have not missed a symbol or counted it more than once.

3.4.2.1   Test Procedure

Test position – standing.

Instruct the child to look at, but not to touch, the symbols in Figure 3.7. Ask '*How many stars do you see?*'

Figure 3.7   Test pattern for visual integration

▶ 3.5 TESTS FOR VISUAL-SPEECH RECOGNITION

3.5.1 SOUND DISCRIMINATION (INDIVIDUAL SOUNDS, SOUND BLENDS AND SYLLABLES)

In order to read, a child must be able to translate a visual symbol on the page to an auditory equivalent. In addition to control of oculomotor skills this requires prior ability to discriminate between different sounds, sound blends and non-sense words such as syllables.

A child's ability to articulate individual sounds clearly and precisely often reflects phonetic and auditory perception. Difficulty with either matching visual symbols to sounds or pronouncing sounds correctly can undermine reading and spelling.

As difficulties on the first three tests for sound discrimination could also arise from visual-perceptual problems, if the child fails the test the first time, repeat the procedure asking the child to repeat each sound after you.

3.5.1.1 Test Procedure

Ask the child to '*Look at these letters and tell me what sound you would make for them*'.

Consonant sounds:	b l j e f p r n d m
Consonant blends:	br sp th fl pr sh ch pl
Syllables:	ate ring ed ow en ly

3.5.1.2 Observations

- Can the child match the letters to the correct sounds on all three tests?
- Does the child start to fail at matching letters to sounds when more than one letter is presented?
- If the child fails at the first part of the test, is he/she able to repeat the sound(s) correctly?

3.5.1.3 Scoring

0. Letters and sounds matched correctly on all three tests.
1. Letters and sounds matched correctly on consonants and blends.
2. Letters and sounds matched correctly on consonants only.
3. Letters and sound matched correctly when asked to repeat the sounds.
4. Unable to match sounds clearly either from reading the symbols or repeating aloud.

If the child is unable to read *and* repeat the sounds correctly, it might indicate the need for referral for a hearing test and possible follow-up. If no abnormality is found on standard hearing tests, then appropriate sound therapy may be indicated.

3.5.2 SOUND SYNTHESIS

Reading, spelling and the ability to follow sequential instructions depend on speed of processing auditory stimuli. Research has demonstrated that children with reading disabilities are often slow at processing the sounds of speech and fail to register individual sounds within a word. Others have difficulty in following sequential instructions because they are still processing the first part of an instruction when the second and third parts are being given. The following test for sound synthesis, originally developed by Valett,[9] can indicate difficulties in perceiving all of the sounds within individual words.

3.5.2.1 Test Procedure

Test position – standing.

Do not allow the child to *see* the following words during this test.

Instruct the child to:

Name the second sound in the word **cat**.
Name which sound in the word **stop** comes after **t**?
What word is made by putting these letters together: **m** then **a** then **n**?
Tell me the names and sounds of the letters in the word **dog**?

3.5.2.2 Scoring

0. All sounds identified and named correctly in the correct sequence.
1. Fails to name the sounds of the letters in the word **dog** in the correctly and in the correct order.
2. Fails to identify the sounds and grouping of the letters which form the word **man** and **dog**.
3. Fails to identify the sound **o** in the word **stop**.
4. Fails to identify any of the above sounds.

If a child above the age of $7^1/_2$ years scores 4 on both the sound discrimination and sound synthesis tests, it is recommended that referral is made for a hearing test and possible additional investigations for auditory processing difficulties.

▶ 3.6 TESTS FOR VISUAL PERCEPTION AND VISUAL-MOTOR INTEGRATION

The following two tests have been adapted from tests for visual perception and visual-motor maturity originally developed by AE Tansley[10] and Lauretta Bender.[11]

The Tansley Standard Figures are based on drawing tests originally devised by Gesell for the assessment of fine motor abilities and visual-perceptual motor skills. There is a developmental age at which a child should be able to copy each of the shapes. Discrepancy between a child's ability to produce an age appropriate drawing and chronological age provides one indication of immaturity in visual-perceptual motor skills.

The Bender Visual Motor Gestalt Test was first developed by child neuropsychiatrist Lauretta Bender in 1938 and published as a monograph, *A visual motor gestalt test and its uses* by The American Othopsychiatric Association. It was designed to evaluate visual-motor maturity, to screen for developmental disorders, or to assess neurological function or brain damage.

The original test consisted of nine figures, each on its own 3 × 5 inch card. The subject was shown each figure and asked to copy it onto a piece of blank paper. The results were scored based on accuracy and other characteristics. Many of the figures used in these tests have been incorporated into other standardised screening tests for visual perception and visual motor integration. In the context of *these* screening tests they should be used for *screening* purposes only to identify signs of difficulty in three areas of functioning. If problems are found to be present, more detailed assessment using one of the following screening tests may be indicated.[‡]

3.6.1 VISUAL PERCEPTION

Visual perception describes the brain's ability to interpret and make sense of visual images seen with the eyes enabling the brain to interpret correctly what is seen. This involves much more than simply adequate eyesight and is the product of multi-sensory and motor experience combined with vision and other information derived from other sensory systems together with operations in space. Visual perception is a compound function. Difficulties with visual perception may be seen in *consistent* misrepresentation of individual figures on the Tansley Standard Figures or shapes and patterns in figures derived from The Bender Visual Motor Gestalt Test.

Examples of visual perceptual difficulties when copying the bottom row of figures from the Tansley Standard Figures (Figure 3.8) may be seen in Figure 3.9 (before starting the developmental movement programme). Figure 3.10 shows drawings by the same child three months after starting a developmental movement programme. When he was shown his first set of drawings his comment was that he had been given different shapes to copy the first time, as they did not look the same as the second set. This is an example of a 'hidden' visual discrimination[**] problem, which cannot necessarily be detected by simply asking a child to match two identical shapes, such as matching a circle with a circle from a test sheet. The child may be able to match similar shapes, but this does not provide information about how the child actually *perceives* the shapes. Examples seen on the triangle, upturned box and diamond in Figure 3.9 show signs of visual discrimination difficulty in the *perception* of acute angles. The union jack figure provides indications of difficulty with visual convergence in perceiving that all lines intersect in the centre.

In addition to visual perceptual problems, Figures 3.9 and 3.10 also show difficulties with visual-motor integration.

3.6.2 VISUAL-MOTOR INTEGRATION (VMI)

Visual-motor integration refers to the ability to coordinate motor movement with a visual stimulus. The child with a difficulty in this area has problems coordinating what he/she sees with an appropriate motor response required in fine motor skills, as, for example, in copying, writing and drawing. VMI involves visual-perception combined with motor coordination to achieve accurate reproduction of the model. Figures 3.9 and 3.10 show difficulties with visual-motor integration with:

- Control of the pencil affecting the quality of the line on all shapes in Figure 3.9.
- Poor closure of shapes at the corners in Figures 3.9 and 3.10.

[‡] Subsequently, the tests were used extensively on military personnel and, in 1964, Elizabeth M. Koppitz produced a new version for clinical use, The Bender-Gestalt Test for Young Children. This has since been revised as **The Koppitz Developmental Scoring System for the Bender-Gestalt Test**. The Bender Gestalt Test was purchased in the 1990s by Riverside Publishing Company and released with a revised qualitative scoring system as the **Bender-II**. The Bender-II contains 16 figures; in the original there were only nine figures.

[**] Visual discrimination describes the ability to see similarities and differences between shapes.

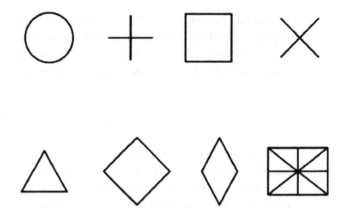

Figure 3.8   The Tansley Standard Figures

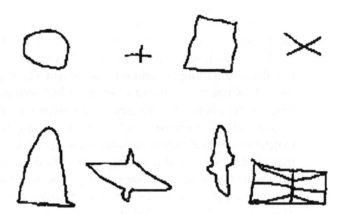

Figure 3.9   First drawing of Tansley Standard Figures

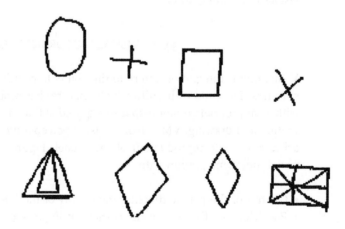

Figure 3.10   Second drawing of Tansley Standard Figures – 3 months later

- Ability to cross the midline with the horizontal and diagonal lines seen on the Union Jack shape in Figure 3.9.
- Continued difficulty with crossing the midline with diagonal lines in Figure 3.10.

3.6.3   SPATIAL DIFFICULTIES

Spatial difficulties may be evident in the size, orientation and layout of figures on the page. Mild spatial problems can be seen in irregularity of the size of shapes in Figure 3.9 and the row of shapes sloping downwards and to the right in Figure 3.10.

3.6.4   THE TANSLEY STANDARD VISUAL FIGURES TEST[10]

Test procedure

Test position – seated at a table.

Observe the child carrying out all drawing tasks.

Present these figures in Figure 3.11 to the child in *landscape* style. Instruct the child to copy these figures **freehand** using a pencil on to a blank sheet of A4 paper. The instruction to the child should make it clear that the copy should look an exact copy of the paper presented.

3.6.5   FIGURES BASED ON THE BENDER VISUAL MOTOR GESTALT TEST[12]

3.6.5.1   Test Procedure

Present these figures in Figure 3.12 to the child in vertical orientation (portrait style) and instruct the child to copy the shapes freehand with a pencil on to a blank sheet of A4 paper.

Observe the child during this drawing task.

The Bender Visual Motor Gestalt figures are usually presented individually to the test subject and are either copied or drawn from memory. INPP has adapted the use of these shapes, presenting them on one page at the same time, to assess how the child copes with multiple visual stimuli.

Figures 3.13 and 3.14 show scaled down examples of severe visual discrimination and visual-motor integration difficulties on the adapted Bender Visual Motor Gestalt figures.

Severe visual perceptual difficulties may be observed on Figure 3.13 in consistent distortion of the upturned box, diamond and hexagonal shapes, together with perseveration of the first shapes (circle and upturned box) on the top row. Shapes that are either conjoined or interlinked on the model are drawn detached from each other and the child is unable to see that the middle row of dots forms an arrow shape.

Figure 3.14 is drawn by the same child five months after starting a twelve-month developmental movement programme. Visual perception is still evident (e.g. separation of the circle and upturned box) but is a marked improvement on her first attempt (Figure 3.13). There are still significant difficulties with visual-motor integration evident in crossing out her first and second attempts at several of the figures. Like the child who drew Figures 3.9 and 3.10, when shown her first drawing (Figure 3.13) she claimed that she must have been given different shapes to copy each time as they did not *look* the same (visual perception), but expressed her frustration at not being able to draw what she could now see as well as she would like (visual-motor integration difficulty).

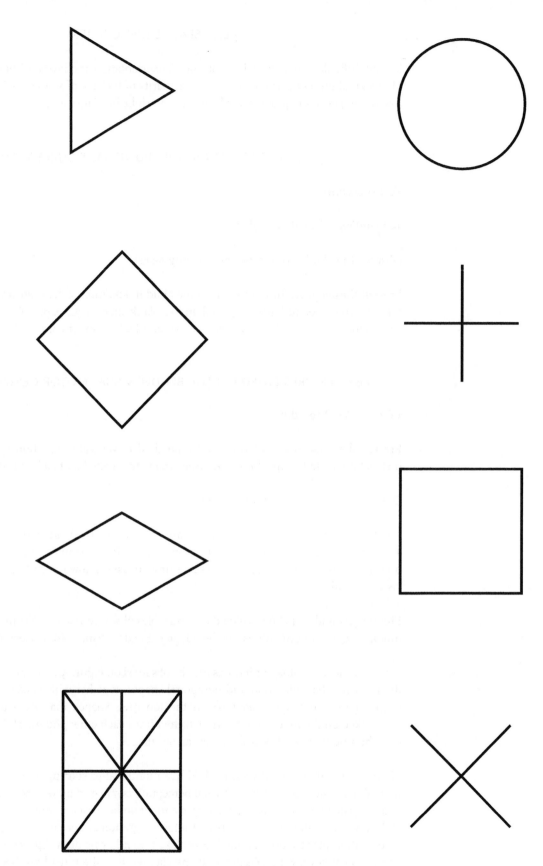

Figure 3.11   Tansley Standard Visual Figures

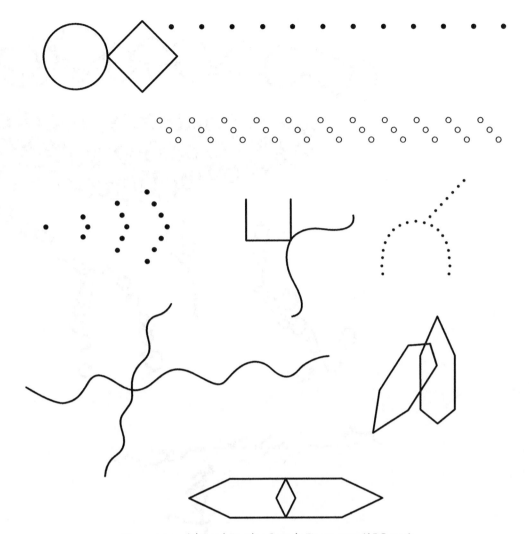

Figure 3.12   Adapted Bender Gestalt Figure test (ABG test)

3.6.6   SCORING THE VISUAL-PERCEPTUAL TESTS

There are specific ages at which a child would be expected to be able to reproduce each of the shapes based on the Tansley Standard Figures:

• Circle	3 years (clockwise)
• Circle	5 years (counter-clockwise)[3]
• Cross	$3^1/_2$ years
• Square	4 years
• X	$4^1/_2$–$5^1/_2$ years
• Triangle	6 years
• Upturned box	7 years
• Diamond	7–$7^1/_2$ years
• Union Jack	6 years

It is therefore possible to identify signs of immaturity in visual perception or visual-motor integration if a child is unable to reproduce shapes which are commensurate with his/her chronological age.

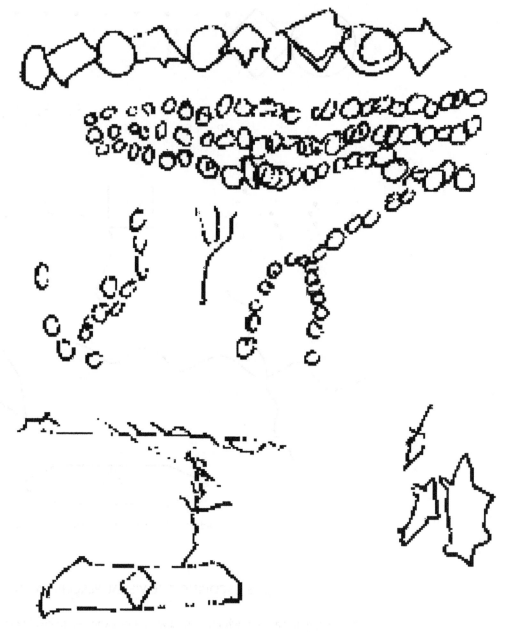

Figure 3.13   ABG Test before intervention

Criteria for assessing visual perception on both tests include:

1. Consistent misrepresentation of the same figure.
2. Reduction or increase of elements, for example, the number of dots on the Bender Visual Motor Gestalt Test (BVMG Test) sheet are fewer or more than shown.
3. Substitution of elements, for example, drawing dots for circles on the BVMG Test sheet.
4. Perseveration (repeating the same shape several times although it is only shown once on the model).
5. Separation of conjoined figures, such as the circle and the square, on the BVMG figures.
6. Inability to perceive shapes and patterns, for example, that the group of dots form an arrow shape.
7. Rotation of figures.

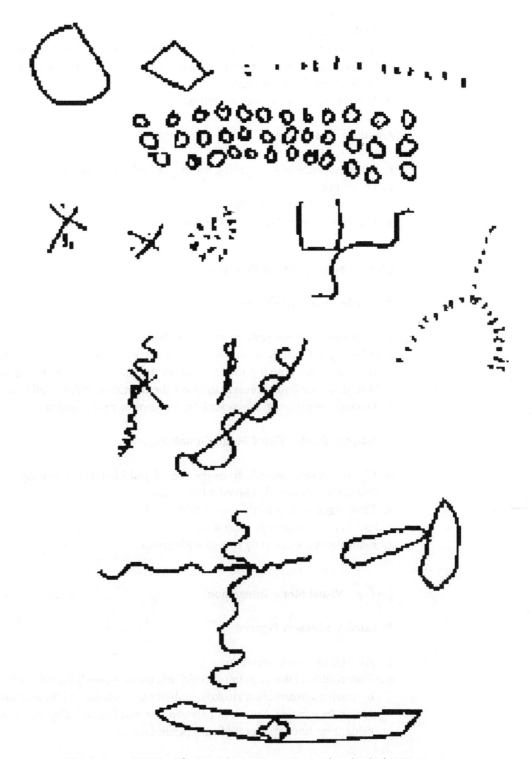

Figure 3.14   ABG Test five months into a 12–18 month individual INPP programme

Criteria for assessing visual-motor integration on both tests:

1. Quality and control of lines, for example, wobbly lines, tremor, use of small approximation strokes.
2. Closure of shapes at the corners.
3. Failure to cross the midline.

4. Inability to control size of individual shapes.
5. Number of correct drawings not commensurate with the chronological age of the child, that is, discrepancy between developmental age and chronological age in representation of the Tansley Standard Figures.
6. Size, spacing and shape of figures.

Additional observations:

1. Sitting posture when carrying out paper and pencil tasks.
2. Pencil grip.
3. Time taken to complete the task.
4. Expresses dissatisfaction with work produced.

3.6.6.1 Scoring: Visual Perception

A: Tansley Standard Figures

0. Figures copied correctly from the model.
1. Difficulty with crossing the midline on the diagonal lines of the Union Jack.
2. Difficulty with crossing the midline on the horizontal lines of the Union Jack.
3. Mild distortion/misrepresentation on the diamond and/or upturned box.
4. Marked distortion/misrepresentation of two or more figures.

B: Adapted Bender Visual Motor Gestalt Figures

0. Figures copied correctly from the model and identical spatial lay out.
1. One figure incorrectly copied with errors.
2. Three figures incorrectly copied with errors.
3. Five figures incorrectly copied with errors.
4. Eight figures incorrectly copied with errors.

3.6.6.2 Visual Motor Integration

A: Tansley Standard Figures

0 All figures copied correctly.
1–4 Poor control of line (e.g. tremor evident), corners poorly joined, vertical lines sloping, use of small approximation strokes, inability to cross the midline or intersect lines on the Union Jack figure. A score of between one and four will depend on *the degree of difficulty* evident on one or several of these criteria.

B: Adapted Bender Visual Gestalt Figures

0 All figures copied correctly.
1–4 Poor control of line (e.g. tremor evident), corners of shapes poorly joined, vertical lines or row of dots sloping, small circles not in pattern formation, use of small approximation strokes, arrow dot shape or 'igloo' not formed into the correct shape, difficulty drawing the hexagonal shapes correctly, or crossing out first attempts.
A score of between one and four will depend on *the degree of difficulty evident on one or several of these criteria.*

3.6.7.1 Draw a Person Test

Children's drawings provide a measure of developmental progress and delay. As early as 1921 Burt[14] had stated that developmental progress and evidence of delay could be observed in children's drawings and, in 1926, Goodenough[15] published findings using the 'Draw A Man Test', which showed that children's drawings are linked to intelligence. Goodenough's test was refined by Harris[16] in 1963, and since that time the scoring system in The Goodenough–Harris Drawing Test has been shown to correlate with intelligence tests such as the Wechsler and Binet scales.

While many factors (visual-motor integration difficulties for example) can contribute to difficulties with the mechanical aspects of drawing, the Draw a Person Test provides *one* measure of nonverbal cognitive performance. A number of scoring systems are available to assess a child's drawing of the human figure. Irrespective of which scoring system is used, a child's drawing of the human figure can provide useful additional information concerning:

- Discrepancy between mental age compared to chronological age or percentile score on the test as *one* measure of nonverbal performance.
- A child's awareness of his/her body image.
- Evidence of neuromotor factors affecting nonverbal performance.

Findings from studies using the INPP Developmental Exercise Programme for use in schools have shown consistent improvement in drawing skills including the Draw a Person Test following intervention.[17] Improvements in nonverbal performance are important because up to 90% of effective communication is based on the nonverbal aspects of language. Nonverbal skills are also linked to visuospatial awareness, which supports many other aspects of learning.

Used in this context, the Draw a Person Test can provide a useful additional tool to identify signs of immaturity in nonverbal performance and to provide an objective measurement of change in nonverbal performance following intervention.

3.6.7.2 Reading Age or National Curriculum Assessment for Reading, Writing and Maths (from Five Years of Age)

Reading age or national curriculum assessment for reading, writing and maths provide additional objective measures of a child's performance on verbal, motor and numerical tasks.

These assessments can either be repeated following intervention or extracted from individual national curriculum records after intervention to evaluate whether improvement in neuro-motor performance crosses over into educational performance. There can be a delay of several months between improvement in neuromotor skills and performance on educational measures.

▶ 3.7   SCORE SHEETS (7 + TEST)

	1st assessment	2nd assessment
Name		
Code		
Gender		
Age		
Date		

Tests for gross muscle coordination, balance and reflexes:		
Tandem walk – forwards	0 1 2 3 4	0 1 2 3 4
Tandem walk – backwards	0 1 2 3 4	0 1 2 3 4
Fog walk – forwards	0 1 2 3 4	0 1 2 3 4
Fog walk backwards	0 1 2 3 4	0 1 2 3 4
Asymmetrical Tonic Neck Reflex Quadruped test – right	0 1 2 3 4	0 1 2 3 4
Asymmetrical Tonic Neck Reflex Quadruped test – left	0 1 2 3 4	0 1 2 3 4
Asymmetrical Tonic Neck Reflex Erect test – right	0 1 2 3 4	0 1 2 3 4
Asymmetrical Tonic Neck Reflex Erect test – left	0 1 2 3 4	0 1 2 3 4
Symmetrical Tonic Neck Reflex – flexion	0 1 2 3 4	0 1 2 3 4
Symmetrical Tonic Neck Reflex – extension	0 1 2 3 4	0 1 2 3 4
Tonic Labyrinthine Reflex – flexion	0 1 2 3 4	0 1 2 3 4
Tonic Labyrinthine Reflex – extension	0 1 2 3 4	0 1 2 3 4
Total	/48	/48

Tests for visual tracking and integration:	1st assessment	2nd assessment
Visual tracking test	0 1 2 3 4	0 1 2 3 4
Visual integration test	0 1 2 3 4	0 1 2 3 4
Total	/8	/8

Auditory–speech recognition tests:	1st assessment	2nd assessment
Consonant sounds	0 1 2 3 4	0 1 2 3 4
Consonant blends	0 1 2 3 4	0 1 2 3 4
Syllables	0 1 2 3 4	0 1 2 3 4
Syntheses	0 1 2 3 4	0 1 2 3 4
Total	/16	/16

Tests for visual perception and visual-motor integration:	1st assessment	2nd assessment
Tansley – visual perception	0 1 2 3 4	0 1 2 3 4
Tansley – visual-motor integration	0 1 2 3 4	0 1 2 3 4
Tansley – spatial	0 1 2 3 4	0 1 2 3 4
Adapted Bender Visual Motor Gestalt – visual perception	0 1 2 3 4	0 1 2 3 4
Adapted Bender Visual Motor Gestalt – visual motor integration	0 1 2 3 4	0 1 2 3 4
Adapted Bender Visual Motor Gestalt – spatial	0 1 2 3 4	0 1 2 3 4
Total	/24	/24

Final Scores	1st assessment	2nd assessment
Gross muscle coordination, balance and reflexes	/48	/48
Visual tracking and integration	/8	/8
Auditory–speech recognition	/16	/16
Visual perception and visual-motor integration	/24	/24
Total (Raw Score)	/96	/96
Percentage Score		

	1st assessment	*2nd assessment*
Name		
Code		
Gender		
Age		
Date		

Tests for gross muscle coordination, balance and reflexes:
Tandem walk – forwards
Tandem walk – backwards
Fog walk – forwards
Fog walk backwards
Asymmetrical Tonic Neck Reflex Quadruped test (right)
Asymmetrical Tonic Neck Reflex Quadruped test (left)
Asymmetrical Tonic Neck Reflex Erect test (right)
Asymmetrical Tonic Neck Reflex Erect test (left)
Symmetrical Tonic Neck Reflex (flexion)
Symmetrical Tonic Neck Reflex (extension)
Tonic Labyrinthine Reflex (flexion)
Tonic Labyrinthine Reflex (extension)

Tests for visual tracking and integration: *1st assessment*   *2nd assessment*
Visual tracking test
Visual integration test

Auditory–speech recognition tests: *1st assessment*   *2nd assessment*
Consonant sounds
Consonant blends
Syllables
Syntheses

Tests for visual perception and visual-motor integration: *1st assessment*   *2nd assessment*
Tansley – visual perception
Tansley – visual-motor integration
Tansley – spatial
Adapted Bender Visual Motor Gestalt – visual perception
Adapted Bender Visual Motor Gestalt – visual motor
  integration
Adapted Bender Visual Motor Gestalt – spatial
Total

▶ 3.9 HOW TO INTERPRET THE SCORES

The final scores have been divided into different sections to identify whether signs of immaturity are more prevalent in one or several areas of functioning.

Scores are interpreted in five categories:

1. **No abnormality detected (NAD)**
2. **Low score**   < 25%
3. **Medium score**   25–50%
4. **High score**   50–75%
5. **Very high score**   75–100%

3.9.1 TESTS FOR GROSS MUSCLE COORDINATION, BALANCE AND REFLEXES

1. **NAD**	No action required.
2. **Low Score**	No action required but child may benefit from participating in the INPP developmental exercise programme.
3. **Medium Score**	INPP developmental exercise programme recommended.
4. **High Score**	INPP developmental exercise programme recommended but additional referral may also be indicated. Children in this group may also benefit from an *individual* reflex integration programme devised by an INPP practitioner following a full neuro-developmental assessment.
5. **Very High Score**	Referral through family doctor for further professional assessment for possible diagnosis and professional intervention or support indicated.

3.9.2 TESTS FOR VISUAL PERCEPTION AND VISUAL-MOTOR INTEGRATION

If scores in this section *and* the section for gross muscle coordination, balance and reflexes range from *medium to high*, improvements will often be seen in visual perception and visual motor integration as neuromotor skills mature following use of the INPP Developmental Movement Programme.

If scores for visual perception and visual motor integration fall anywhere in the low to very high range, *with* scores for gross muscle coordination, balance and reflexes falling within the normal range, referral to an optometrist for a full vision test is recommended. If vision is normal when tested at far and near distance, but problems are still evident on tests for visual perception *without abnormal reflexes being evident,* it *may* indicate an oculomotor dysfunction. Further assessment by an orthoptist is recommended.

3.9.3 TESTS FOR AUDITORY–SPEECH RECOGNITION

If scores in this section fall *between the medium and very high range,* it is recommended that the child is referred for audiometric assessment. If audiometric tests are normal but problems are still evident in discriminating between different sounds or in following sequences of information, these difficulties *might* indicate an auditory *processing* difficulty. Referral for further investigations for auditory processing *disorder* or auditory processing *difficulties* may be recommended.

Auditory processing *disorder*, which may also be referred to as central auditory processing disorder (CAPD), auditory perception problem, auditory comprehension deficit, central auditory dysfunction, central deafness, or so-called 'word deafness' can be made following referral by a doctor and diagnosed following audiological examination by an audiologist and assessment by a speech and language pathologist.

Auditory processing *difficulties* can be identified and treated with the use of appropriate sound therapy. A number of methods of sound therapy are available, some of which can be applied in school or at home (Johansen Individualized Auditory Stimulation (JIAST), The Listening Program (TLP), The LiFT Program or Musica Medica). Others require treatment at a centre specialising in the method (The Tomatis Method, Auditory Integrative Training (AIT), Musica Medica). Details of different methods of sound therapy listed above can be found in the resources section at the end of Chapter 4.

▶ REFERENCES

[1] Hoff, H and Schilder, P (1927) *Der Lagereflexe des Menschen. Klinische Untersuchungen über Haltungs- und Stellreflexe und verwandte Phänomene.* Julius Springer, Vienna, Austria.

[2] Fog, E and Fog, M (1963) Cerebral inhibition examined by associated movements. In: MacKeith, R and Bax, M (eds), Minimal cerebral dysfunction. Papers from the International Study Group, Oxford, September 1962. William Heinemann Medical Books Ltd, London

[3] Accardo, PJ (1980) *A neuro-developmental perspective on specific learning difficulties.* University Park Press, Baltimore, MD.

[4] Goddard, SA (2002) *Reflexes, learning and behaviour. A window into the child's mind.* Fern Ridge Press, Eugene, OR.

[5] Ayres, AJ (1978) *Sensory integration and learning disorders.* Western Psychological Services, Los Angeles, CA.

[6] Parmentier, CL (1975) The asymmetrical tonic neck reflex in normal first and third grade children. *The American Journal of Occupational Therapy*, **29**(8): 463–468.

[7] Silver, AA (1952) Postural and righting responses in children. *J. Pediatr.*, **41**: 493–498

[8] McPhillips, M and Jordan Black, JA (2007) Primary reflex persistence in children with reading difficulties (dyslexia): A cross-sectional study, *Neuropsychologia.*, **45**: 748–754.

[9] Valett, RE (1980) *Dyslexia – a neurophysiological approach.* Costello Educational, Tunbridge Wells.

[10] Tansley, AE (1967) *Reading and remedial reading.* Routledge and Kegan Paul Ltd, London.

[11] Bender, L (1938) *A visual motor gestalt test and its clinical uses.* American Ortho-psychiatric Association, New York.

[12] Brannigan, G and Decker, S (2003) *Bender visual-motor gestalt test*, 2nd edn *(Bender gestalt II).* Western Psychological Services, Los Angeles, CA.

[13] Reynolds, CR (2007) *The Koppitz developmental scoring system for the Bender gestalt test*, 2nd edn. Western Psychological Services, Los Angeles, CA.

[14] Burt, C (1921) *Mental and scholastic tests.* PS King & Son, London.

[15] Goodenough, F (1926) *Measurement of intelligence by drawings.* Yonkers-on-Hudson, World Book Co., New York.

[16] Harris, DB (1963) *Children's drawings as measures of intellectual maturity.* Harcourt, Brace & World, Inc., New York.

[17] Goddard Blythe, SA (2005) Releasing educational potential through movement. A summary of individual studies carried out using the INPP Test Battery and Developmental Exercise Programme for use in schools with children with special needs. *Child Care in Practice*, **11**(4): 415–432.

4

The INPP Developmental Movement Programme

▶ 4.1 HOW TO USE THE INPP DEVELOPMENTAL MOVEMENT PROGRAMME

The INPP Developmental Movement Programme involves carrying out a series of developmental movements each day, based on movements normally made by the developing child in the first year of life.

Key elements of the programme are:

1. Regularity (every school day).
2. Repetition (repeating the same movements over a period of several weeks).
3. Duration (minimum of 9 months and preferably 12 months).

Time required:

- 15 minutes per day.

Space and equipment required:

- School hall, gymnasium or similar space.
- Gym mat or clean towel for children to lie on.
- Children do not need to change into PE (physical education/gym) clothes but should remove shoes and socks.

Staffing requirement:

- One member of staff who has either attended an INPP training course or read the instruction manual and followed the video training.
- When using the programme with children under seven years of age, or with a class of mixed ability, additional support staff may be needed to help children with more severe difficulties.

Assessing Neuromotor Readiness for Learning: The INPP Developmental Screening Test and School Intervention Programme, First Edition. Sally Goddard Blythe.
© 2012 John Wiley & Sons, Ltd. Published 2012 by John Wiley & Sons, Ltd.

Contra-indications to using the programme

Please note: if a child has a medical condition likely to affect physical coordination or is currently receiving treatment from a doctor or therapist for a physical condition, check with the therapist that there are no contra-indications to the child participating in the INPP developmental movement programme.

Supporting video material showing examples of all of the exercises may be found at www.accessnmr.inpp.org.uk. Registration on the site will provide one month's free access to all material.

4.1.1   DEVELOPMENTAL MOVEMENTS

The majority of exercises are carried out on the floor. They aim to develop correct head alignment with the body (the basis for good posture), and the ability to use the left and right sides and upper and lower sections of the body in different ways (the basis for coordination). Only when every child in the group can carry out the earliest simple movements with automaticity does the group move on to repeat the movements in more challenging positions. When using the programme with children over seven years of age, all movements should be carried out *as slowly as possible* allowing a few seconds pause between each phase of the exercise.

4.1.2   WHY USE A MOVEMENT PROGRAMME TO IMPROVE EDUCATIONAL PERFORMANCE?

Movement is a child's first language, and it is through the medium of movement that he/she first starts to explore the world and to gain control over his/her body. The most advanced level of movement is the ability to stay totally still[1] and until a child has control of balance and the ability to sit or to stand still, he/she does not have the physical equipment necessary to support learning in the classroom.

Motor development during the first year of life should follow a strict chronological sequence which is roughly the same for every child irrespective of race or culture. For example, before a child can gain good control of the rest of his/her body, he/she must first attain head control. Normal development follows a cephalo-caudal (from head to toe) and proximo-distal (from the centre outwards) sequence. Within this general framework a more detailed pattern emerges.

Development on the stomach is more precocious than development on the back (provided a child is placed on its front when awake in the first year of life). The developing child progresses from total body movements, where flexion, extension or rotation of the head is accompanied by reflexive movement of the limbs, to independent head movement, the ability to bring one side of the body to the midline, and eventually to cross the midline. The ability to cross the midline is essential for fluent cross-pattern movements to develop. The child must also learn to move his/her head forwards and backwards without inducing involuntary flexion or extension of other muscle groups. Control of the balance between flexor and extensor muscle tone begins at the head and gradually works down to the trunk, and also works its way up from the feet to the trunk. Truncal integration starts to develop from about 4 to 8 months of age, enabling the baby to roll using rotation through the middle section of the body. Ideally, all of these stages should have been accomplished before a child is ready to crawl. Crawling begins from the stomach (like a commando), progressing to hands and knees a few weeks later.

The Developmental Movement Programme uses natural movements in a developmental sequence, helping coordination to become an integrated function rather than simply a practice-learned skill. (Skills that are dependent on continuous practice tend to lack flexibility and do not necessarily adapt well or transfer to new situations.)

4.1.3   INSTRUCTIONS FOR USE OF THE EXERCISES

- Exercises to be carried out daily in school for a minimum period of 9–12 months. The exercises may be carried over to a fourth term if required.
- Exercises should always be supervised by a member of staff who has read the manual, followed training on the DVD, or undergone an INPP approved training course in the use of the programme.
- The programme always begins with the 'Windmills' exercise. This is the only exercise which will be used throughout the programme.
- As far as possible, exercises carried out in the prone position should be paired with an exercise which is carried out on the back. The maximum number of floor-based exercises to be used at one time is four (two prone and two supine) in addition to 'Windmills'.
- Floor exercises should be performed **as slowly as possible** with children from seven years of age and upwards.
- When using the programme with children under seven years of age, the exercises may be performed faster, and the number of repetitions increased. Alternatively, to help younger children slow the exercises down, a story is available to accompany the exercises.*
- The floor-based exercises have been designed to be used in blocks of 2–4 exercises for a minimum period of six weeks for each block.
- Only when one block of exercises has been mastered and practised for six weeks, should the group move on to a new block of exercises. This can be done either by:
    a) taking on four new exercises and dropping the previous four exercises; or
    b) retaining two of the most recent exercises and adding two new ones.
The precise amount of time used for each block of exercises should be tailored to the needs of the group. More than six weeks can be allowed for earlier exercises if required.
- The group should **not** move on to new exercises until earlier ones have been completely mastered and practised.
- Teachers should **not** attempt to select individual exercises for particular children, but should follow through the sequence in developmental order as outlined in the manual.
- Table 4.1 is intended **only** as a **guideline** for progress through the exercises.
- The time span for each set of exercises in the guideline can be adjusted according to the needs of the group.

4.1.4   GUIDELINES FOR SCHEDULE FOR EXERCISES

- Arrange a daily 15 minute session to do the exercises.
- Table 4.1 illustrates a typical programme (intended as a **guideline only**) for progress through the exercises if 4 + terms are available.
- First assessment is made using the age-appropriate INPP Screening Test.
- Second assessment is made using the same INPP Screening Test.
- Bilateral integration exercises for an additional term if required.

---

* Early Morning by the Pond. Published in *The Well Balanced Child* by Sally Goddard Blythe (2004). Hawthorn Press, Stroud, UK.

Table 1. Guideline for progress through the exercises

First 4 weeks	Windmill, Caterpillar, Sea Anemone
4–8 weeks	Windmill, Sea Anemone, Caterpillar, Curious Caterpillar
8–14 weeks	Windmill, Sea Anemone, Curious Caterpillar, Parachute, Octopus 1
14–20 weeks	Windmill, Agitated Caterpillar, Parachute, Octopus 1, Octopus 2
20–26 weeks	Windmill, Parachute, Head Lift, Fish 1, Octopus 2
26–32 weeks	Windmill, Fish 2, Lizard, The Hinge
32–38 weeks	Windmill Lizard, the Bracket, Hand to Foot, Hand to Knee
38–42 weeks	Windmill, Lower Body Rotation, Upper Body Rotation
42–46 weeks	Windmill, Full Body Rotation combined, the Tadpole, the Drunken Frog
46–50 weeks	Windmill, the Drunken Frog, (the Alligator), the Commando Crawl, the Cat
50–54 weeks	Windmill, (the Cat), 3-point Pattern Creeping
54–58 weeks	Cross-Pattern Crawling on Hands and Knees
58–70 weeks	(Additional exercises for bilateral integration if required)

▶ 4.2   THE DEVELOPMENTAL MOVEMENT PROGRAMME

4.2.1   INTRODUCTION

The exercises listed in Table 4.1 are described in detail in the following sections.

Start each session with a general 'warming up' exercise each day, such as jogging on the spot, moving the arms and the legs. Progress to jogging around the room, until 'warmed up'. Vary the warming up exercise every few days.

4.2.2   WINDMILLS[2]

Stand with arms stretched out at shoulder level on each side (Figure 4.1).

Slowly turn round in a complete circle until facing the same point at which you started.

Stand still with your feet together.

Close your eyes and put your arms down to your sides.

Stand still for 15 seconds keeping your eyes closed.

Open your eyes, extend your arms to the sides; slowly turn in a complete circle in the opposite direction.

Figure 4.1

Close your eyes and stand still with your feet together; put your arms down by your sides; stand still for a further 15 seconds.

As balance improves when standing still with the eyes closed, the number and speed of rotations in each direction may be increased before the period of standing still with eyes closed.

Exactly the same number of rotations should be made in each direction, and there should always be a 15 second pause with the eyes closed before changing direction. This allows the balance mechanism to stabilise, without depending on visual input for the child to gauge where he/she is in space.

If working with younger children (under $6^1/_2$ years), both speed and number of rotations may be increased, but the programme should always be started with the minimum number of rotations.

Alternatively, if younger children find it difficult to maintain balance after only one rotation, it may be necessary to build up to one rotation gradually. For example, starting with a quarter turn, followed by a stop, eyes closed, feet together, arms down by the sides, 15 second pause. Open the eyes, extend the arms to the sides, return to starting position, feet together, close the eyes; arms down by the sides and pause for 15 seconds.

This should then be followed by a quarter turn to the opposite side and repeat the sequence.

Once children have mastered a quarter turn in each direction (usually about two weeks), this can be increased to a half turn in each direction (further two weeks), then a three quarter turn (two weeks) until all children can manage one complete rotation in each direction and the period of standing still with the eyes closed without loss of balance.

Exercises performed on the back should be accompanied by an equal number of exercises carried out on the front

4.2.3 CATERPILLAR

Lie on the front with legs straight and arms bent at the elbows, tucked in at the sides of the body (Figure 4.2), palms of the hands flat on the floor and thumbs abducted (Figure 4.3).

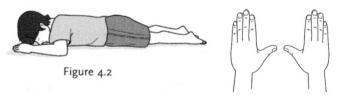

Figure 4.2

Figure 4.3

Slowly lift the head until the back of the head is level with the spine (this is only a distance of 4–5 inches off the ground) (Figure 4.4).

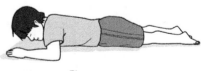

Figure 4.4

The child may need a helper or partner to place a hand at the top of the spine in order to 'feel' the correct position for alignment of the head with the body.

The head should not be tilted back or above the level of the body.

Hold the head up in line with the body for 3–5 seconds.

Slowly lower the head down to the starting position on the ground (Figure 4.5).

Figure 4.5

Pause for 3–5 seconds.

Repeat the sequence up to six times.

4.2.4 THE CURIOUS CATERPILLAR

Starting position as for the caterpillar (Figure 4.6).

Figure 4.6

Lift the head to the level of the spine; keeping the head in line with the spine, push with the arms, raising the chest off the ground until resting on the forearms.

Keep the palms of the hands flat on the ground, fingers together and thumb abducted (Figure 4.7).

Figure 4.7

Hold this position for 3–5 seconds (the children may count aloud).

Slowly lower the chest to the ground, keeping the head in line with the back, and then lower the head to the ground as in the previous exercise (Figure 4.8).

Figure 4.8

Pause for 3–5 seconds.

Repeat the sequence up six times.

4.2.5 THE SEA ANEMONE

Lie on the back, curled up with the arms crossed, each hand resting on the opposite shoulder, and also with the legs crossed at the ankles and the head off the ground (Figure 4.9). (The child may require support under the head.)

Figure 4.9

Note: The same arm and leg should be uppermost.

Close the eyes.

Slowly (as if looking at a slow motion film of a flower opening out of bud), tilt the head back and lower the head until it is resting on the ground. *At the same time,* slowly open out the arms and the legs keeping them slightly flexed and off the ground (Figure 4.10).

Figure 4.10

Pause in this position for five seconds and then slowly curl back into the starting position, bringing the head up as the arms and legs curl in to cross-over (Figure 4.11).

Repeat the sequence once more.

Figure 4.11

Once the group has mastered control of the head and the opening and closing movement, instruct them to change the uppermost arm and leg each time they curl up into the closed position. For example, right arm and leg uppermost the first time, left arm and leg uppermost the second time and so on.

4.2.6   THE OCTOPUS (PART 1)

Lie on the back, with arms and legs straight, palms of the hands flat on the floor (Figure 4.12).

Figure 4.12

Slowly splay the fingers and toes, stretching them as far as possible (Figure 4.13).

Pause for 3–5 seconds.

Repeat six times

Relax.

Figure 4.13

Curl the fingers, with the thumb over the top of the fingers, and curl the toes at the same time.

Hold this position for 3–5 seconds (Figure 4.14).

Figure 4.14

Repeat curling of the fingers and toes followed by relaxation six times.

4.2.7   THE AGITATED CATERPILLAR

Starting position as for the Caterpillar (Figure 4.15).

Slowly bend one leg up to 90° from the floor extending the foot and pointing the first toe.

Figure 4.15

Pause for three seconds (Figure 4.16).

Return first leg to the floor; raise the other leg.

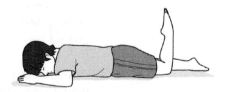

Pause for three seconds.

Alternate the legs.

Figure 4.16

Increase and vary the speed of the movements.

With one leg raised, bring the other leg up so both legs are raised; as slowly as possible, lower both legs until the feet are resting on the floor.

When this is well coordinated, rise up into the 'Curious Caterpillar' position, and carry out leg movements as above in the raised position. (Figures 4.17 and 4.18).

Figure 4.17

Figure 4.18

4.2.8   THE PARACHUTE

Lie on the front with legs straight and arms bent at the elbows on each side of the body. The arms should have a slightly wider base than for the Caterpillar exercises above, the forearms being placed about 5 inches (13 cm) away from the body on either side (Figure 4.19).

Figure 4.19

Lift the head, chest and arms off the ground, and at the same time, elevate the feet approximately 5 inches (13 cm) above the ground.

Hold the raised position for up to five seconds (Figure 4.20)

Figure 4.20

(It is recommended that you ask the group to count the five seconds aloud in the elevated position, to make sure they continue to breathe normally in this position.)

Return to resting position (Figure 4.21).

Figure 4.21

Pause for five seconds in the resting position.

Repeat the sequence up to six times.

4.2.9   THE OCTOPUS (PART 2)

Lie on your back; bend the knees and place the feet flat on the floor; arms straight down by the sides; palms of the hands on the floor; eyes open.

Slowly bend one arm until the forearm and palm of the hand are facing upwards; pause for three seconds and then reach, taking the arm above the head and stretching until the arm is as straight as possible, in line with the body with the fingers extended (Figure 4.22).

Pause for three seconds.

Slowly return the arm to its starting position.

Figure 4.22

This should be repeated with the other arm using the following *sequence* of movements:

1. Bend the arm so the forearm and palm of the hand are facing upwards.
2. Pause for three seconds.
3. Straighten the arm and reach above the head, so that the palm of the hand is facing upwards and the fingers are extended.
4. Pause for three seconds.
5. Bend the arm down to the half-way point (stage 2).
6. Pause for three seconds.
7. Bend the forearm down until the whole arm is resting on the ground with the palm of the hand facing down.
8. Pause for three seconds.

Slowly follow stages 1–4 above, with the other arm.

Pause for three seconds (Figure 4.23).

Figure 4.23

After one week, continue the exercise with the eyes *closed*.

After approximately four weeks, or when all members of the group can carry out the movement one side at a time, instruct the children to:

1. Bend the arm to the half-way point.
2. Pause.
3. Straighten the arm and reach above the head.
4. Pause.
5. Bend the first arm down to the half-way point and *at the same time* bend the other arm up to the half-way point (both arms should be bent by the sides of the body with palms of the hands facing up).
6. Pause.
7. Bend the first arm down to its starting position and, *at the same time*, extend and reach above the head with the second arm.
8. Pause.
9. Bend the straight arm *down* to the half-way point and, *at the same time*, bend the other arm *up* to the half-way point (both arms should be bend by the sides of the body with palms of hands facing up).
10. Pause.
11. Repeat the sequence up to 20 times in slow motion.
12. When all children have mastered the sequence with the eyes open, continue to use the exercise with the eyes closed.

4.2.10   THE HEAD LIFT

Lie on the back with knees bent and feet on the floor.

The arms can rest at the sides of the body, or across the chest.

Slowly lift the head up off the floor as if to look between the knees (Figure 4.24).

Figure 4.24

Pause in this position for three seconds.

Slowly lower the head to the floor.

Pause for three seconds.

Repeat several times.

4.2.11   THE FISH

Lie on the front, with legs straight and arms in 'The Caterpillar' position, forehead resting on the floor. (Figure 4.25).

Figure 4.25

Lift one hip slightly off the ground and allow the knee to flex slightly on the elevated side of the body. (Figure 4.26).

Keep the other leg straight and the head in the middle.

Figure 4.26

Pause for three seconds.

Return to the starting position (Figure 4.27).

Pause for three seconds.

Figure 4.27

Repeat the movement on the other side of the body.

Pause for three seconds.

Repeat the sequence, alternating from side to side, always ensuring that only one side of the lower body is flexed.

(Some children may be able to do it on one side, but need help on the other.)

When this can be done easily, raise up into the 'Curious Caterpillar' position, and repeat the 'Fish' movements, keeping upper portion of the body still, and flexing one knee at a time (Figure 4.28).

Figure 4.28

4.2.12   THE LIZARD

Lie on the front with legs straight and arms bent at the elbows, resting on the forearms (Caterpillar position) (Figure 4.29).

Figure 4.29

Slowly turn the head to the right and, as the head turns, slide the right elbow a little way down towards the waist, and bend the right knee upwards towards the waist (Figure 4.30).

Figure 4.30

Pause for three seconds.

Return to starting position (Figure 4.31).

Figure 4.31

Repeat the same movement to the left, that is, rotate the head to the left and slide the left elbow downwards towards the waist, and bend the left knee upwards towards the waist (Figure 4.32).

Figure 4.32

Pause for three seconds.

Return to the starting position (Figure 4.33).

Repeat the sequence several times.

Figure 4.33

4.2.13   HAND TO FOOT

Lie on the back with the arms and legs straight (Figure 4.34).

Figure 4.34

Lift the head up and, at the same time, bend the right leg at the knee and reach with the right hand to touch the outer side of the right foot (Figure 4.35).

Return to the starting position.

Figure 4.35

Lift the head up, bend the left leg at the knee and reach with the left hand to touch the outer side of the left foot. Repeat until a sequence is established alternating from one side to the other (Figure 4.36).

When this can be done easily, reach with the right hand to touch the inner side of the left foot and vice versa (cross pattern) (Figures 4.37 and 4.38).

Figure 4.36

Figure 4.37

Figure 4.38

Repeat the movement sequence up to six times.

4.2.14   HAND TO KNEE

Lie on the back with arms and legs straight (Figure 4.39).

Figure 4.39

Lift the head off the ground, bend the right leg at the knee and reach with the right hand to touch the right knee (Figure 4.40).

Return to starting position.

Figure 4.40

Repeat the movement using the left knee and left hand (Figure 4.41).

Repeat alternate sides up to six times.

Figure 4.41

When this has been mastered, repeat the movement using the right hand with the left knee and vice versa. (Figure 4.42).

Figure 4.42

4.2.15   THE HINGE

Lie on the back with the body in a straight line; arms and legs straight (Figure 4.43).

Figure 4.43

Slowly rotate the head to one side until the chin is parallel with the shoulder. As the head starts to turn, slowly bend the arm and leg on the side to which the head is turning, and ask the child to follow the movement of the thumb with the eyes for as long as possible (Figure 4.44).

Figure 4.44

(It may be helpful for children to draw smiley faces onto the thumb joint of each hand to make it easier to follow.)

Pause for three seconds.

Slowly return the head to the midline, straightening the arm and leg at the same time and following the movement of the thumb with the eyes for as long as possible (Figure 4.45).

Figure 4.45

Pause for three seconds.

Repeat the movement to the opposite side (Figure 4.46).

Figure 4.46

Repeat the whole sequence 2–3 times.

4.2.16   THE BRACKET

Lie on the back with the body straight (Figure 4.47).

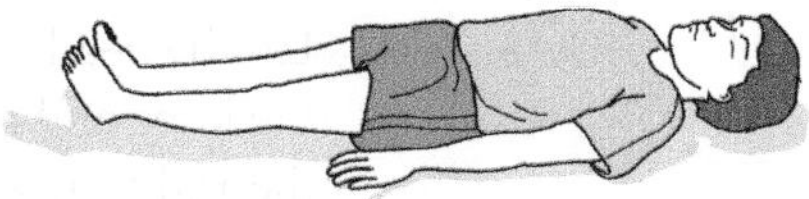

Slowly rotate the head to the right, flex the right arm and the left leg (Figure 4.48).

Figure 4.47

Pause for 2–3 seconds.

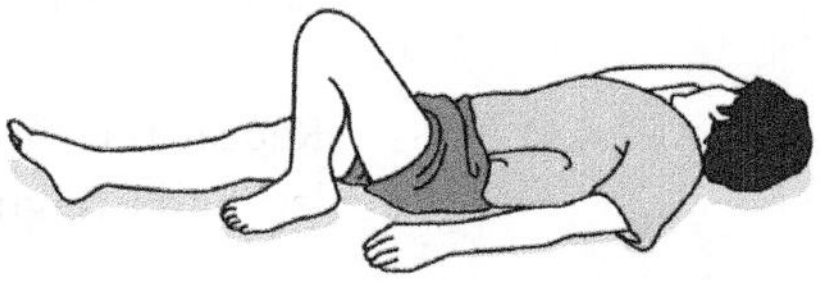

Return the head, arm and leg to the midline (Figure 4.49).

Slowly rotate the head to the left, flex the left arm and the right leg.

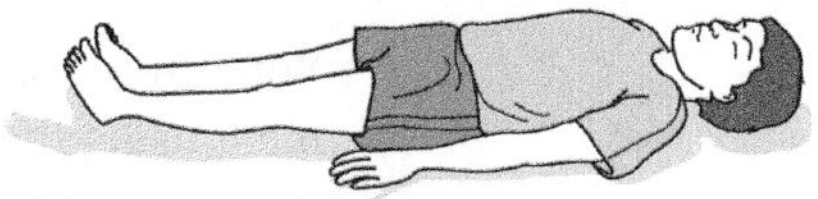

Pause for 2–3 seconds (Figure 4.50).

Figure 4.48

Figure 4.49

Figure 4.50

Return to the midline, and repeat the entire sequence once more.

4.2.17   LOWER BODY ROTATION

Lie on the back with the body in a straight line; legs straight and arms straight down by the sides (Figure 4.51).

Figure 4.51

Slowly turn the head to the left.

Bend the right leg at the knee, keeping the thigh aligned with the body.

Slowly take the knee across the centre of the body as far as is comfortably possible beyond the position indicated in (Figure 4.52).

Figure 4.52

Pause for three seconds.

Return to the starting position
(Figure 4.53)

Figure 4.53

Repeat with the movements to the other side
(Figure 4.54).

Pause for three seconds.

Figure 4.54

Return to the starting position (Figure 4.55).

Repeat the sequence six times.

Figure 4.55

4.2.18   UPPER BODY ROTATION

Lie on the back, with the body straight (Figure 4.56).

Figure 4.56

Rotate the head to the **right** and bring the **left** arm across the body until the hand reaches the right shoulder (Figure 4.57).

Figure 4.57

Pause for three seconds.

Return the head and arm to the midline (Figure 4.58).

Figure 4.58

Rotate the head to the **left** and bring the **right** arm across the body until it reaches the left shoulder (Figure 4.59).

Figure 4.59

Return the head and arm to the midline (Figure 4.60).

Rotate the head to the **right**, and this time bring the **left** knee across the body and allow the **left** arm to follow as the knee crosses over the midline of the body. This should facilitate the beginning of a sequential roll.

Figure 4.60

Return to the starting position (Figure 4.61).

Repeat the sequence to the other side.

Return to the starting position.

Repeat the sequence three times to each side.

Figure 4.61

4.2.19 THE TADPOLE WHO TURNS INTO A FROG

Lie on the front in the 'Curious Caterpillar' position (Figure 4.62).

Turn the head to one side; *at the same time* bend the knee and arm on the same side, twisting the upper section of the body until resting on one side supported by the opposite forearm. Turn the head and the shoulder a little further, as if looking over the opposite shoulder (Figure 4.63).

Pause for three seconds.

Return to the starting position (Figure 4.64).

Turn the head to the opposite side, bending the knee and arm on the same side, turning the upper section of the body until resting on the side supported by the opposite forearm (Figure 4.65).

Pause for three seconds.

Return to the starting position (Figure 4.66).

Practice this movement to either side for at least two weeks.

When this manoeuvre has been mastered to each side, continue to push with the supporting arm and leg and carry on turning until the body turns over in a sequential movement.

The child should turn from prone to arrive in a sitting position, supported by one arm and with the other leg crossed at the ankle (Figure 4.67).

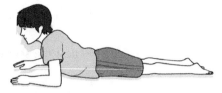

Figure 4.62

Figure 4.63

Figure 4.64

Figure 4.65

Figure 4.66

Figure 4.67

Return to the starting position (Figure 4.68)

Repeat the sequence in the opposite direction (Figure 4.69).

Repeat the sequence to each side several times.

Figure 4.68

Figure 4.69

4.2.20   THE DRUNKEN FROG

Sit on the floor with knees bent and feet on the floor. Support with one hand on the floor to the side of the body. Find an object at eye level to focus on.

Straighten the arm on the other side of the body and shift the support from one side to the other in a sideways rocking motion, so that one hand is on the ground and the other in the air with the body tilted to one side (like an aeroplane changing course) (Figure 4.70).

Figure 4.70

*At the same time,*try to maintain visual focus on the object at eye level while the body is moving, so that the head adjusts to the midline irrespective of the position of the body.

Get the children to work in pairs, sitting facing each other, feet to feet and holding hands.

Instruct them to carry out 'rowing' movements, rocking forwards and backwards as if rowing a boat together.

4.2.21   THE ALLIGATOR

Please note this exercise should *not* be practised for several weeks. Once children are able to perform the actions in a coordinated manner, move on to the Commando Crawl (Exercise 4.2.22).

Lie on the front; reach forward with one arm, and bend the leg on the same side.

Bend the toes of the flexed leg into the ground and push forwards, while reaching with the arm on the same side and making sure the stomach remains in contact with the floor all the time (Figure 4.71).

Figure 4.71

Slowly reach forward with the other arm, bending the leg on the same side as the reaching arm and push forwards with the toes of the flexed leg.

When children have demonstrated they are able to carry out this sequence of movements, do not continue to repeat the exercise. Move immediately on to Exercise 4.2.22.

4.2.22 THE COMMANDO CRAWL

The key feature to this sequence is that forward movement occurs as a result of diagonal coordination through the body, bending of the lower part of the body on one side while straightening the upper part of the body on the same side (cross pattern). Children who have not been able to master earlier exercises in the sequence should not attempt cross-pattern crawling.

Lie on the front. Reach forward with one arm, and bend the leg on the opposite side. Push forward using the toes of the flexed leg while reaching with the opposite arm. Start this sequence as if in slow motion (Figure 4.72).

Figure 4.72

(Many children will need to 'think' each movement and as soon as they speed it up may revert to homolateral (alligator) style crawling. This stage may need several weeks of slow daily practise until it becomes fluent and synchronised.)

If necessary, break the exercise down so that children make one forward movement and then **pause** for a few seconds before changing sides.

After a few weeks of using the cross pattern movement with a pause in the middle, children can be encouraged to develop synchronised crawling by asking them to move forwards in time to a metronome set at a slow speed.

4.2.23 THE CAT

(a) Lie on the front in the 'Curious Caterpillar' position (Figure 4.73)

(b) Resting on the forearms, bend the head down and raise the bottom off the ground (Figure 4.74).

Figure 4.73

Figure 4.74

(c) Raise the head up, keeping the arms straight; allow the arms to slide back and let the bottom sink back on to the ankles (the sitting cat position) (Figure 4.75).

Pause for five seconds.

(d) Slowly bend the head forwards and push with the back legs until the head is level with the spine and the body is in the 'table' position (Figure 4.76).

(e) Raise the head up a little way and continue to push with the back legs until in the 'extended table' position (Figure 4.77).

Figure 4.75

Figure 4.76

Figure 4.77

(f) Carry out a slow rocking movement, starting from the 'extended table' position (e), lowering the head and rocking back until the bottom is on the ankles (Figure 4.78).

(g) Slowly raise the head and rock forwards until in the 'extended table' position (Figures 4.79 and 4.80). Continue slowly rocking forwards and backwards, always pausing for five seconds in positions (e) and (f) (Figures 4.81–4.84 and 4.85)

Figure 4.78

Figure 4.79

Figure 4.80

Figure 4.81

Figure 4.82

Figure 4.83

Figure 4.84

Figure 4.85

4.2.24 THREE-POINT CRAWLING ON HANDS AND KNEES

Assume the four-point kneeling 'table' position.

Three-point crawling on hands and knees means that there are always three balance (support) points firmly on the ground, and only one hand or knee lifted off the ground at a time.

Leading with the right hand, *followed* by the left knee, then left hand *followed* by the right knee start to crawl forwards, always turning the head to follow the leading hand with the eyes.

(A left-handed child may start the sequence with the left hand leading first.)

Beware that the child does not revert to one sided crawling on hands and knees after a few movements, that is, right arm-right leg, left arm-left leg. If this occurs, slow down the sequence, or return to earlier exercises.

It can help to place different coloured stickers on each hand and knee and tell the children to follow a verbal instruction sequence: *'blue (1), orange (2), red (3), yellow (4)'; 'blue (1), orange (2), red (3), yellow (4)'* and so on (Figure 4.86).

Figure 4.86

4.2.25   CROSS-PATTERN CRAWLING ON HANDS AND KNEES

Assume the four-point kneeling 'table' position.

Leading with the right arm, together with the left leg, start to crawl forwards, always turning the head to follow the leading hand with the eyes. A synchronised cross-pattern movement should develop, that is, right hand, left leg, left hand, right leg, and so on. (A left-handed child may start the sequence with the left hand leading first.) Beware that the child does not revert to one sided crawling after a few movements, that is, right arm-right leg, left arm-left leg. If this occurs, slow down the sequence, or return to earlier exercises (Figure 4.87).

Figure 4.87

As in Exercise 4.2.24, coloured stickers can be placed on each hand and knee (stickers using only *two* different colours). For example, a blue sticker on the right hand and right knee and a yellow sticker on the left hand and left knee. Children are then instructed to move following the verbal instruction, *'blue hand and yellow knee; yellow hand and blue knee. Blue hand and yellow knee; yellow hand and blue knee'* and so on.

▶ 4.3   ADDITIONAL OPTIONAL EXERCISES FOR INTEGRATION OF LEFT AND RIGHT

If, following completion of the all of the above exercises, teachers consider that children need additional training in improving left–right (bilateral) integration, the following exercises may be used for a further 6–10 weeks.

Please note that this section of exercises should **not** be used before or during the main exercise programme, as postural control and balance precede bilateral integration in normal development.

The following sample of exercises for training bilateral integration is included with the permission of Sheila Dobie, formerly Director of INPP Scotland.[3,4]

(A full programme of exercises for training bilateral integration developed by Sheila Dobie is available from The Movement and Learning Centre in Scotland.[†])

4.3.1   DIFFERENTIATED ANGELS IN THE SNOW

(Originally created by Kephart, adapted by Dobie, 1996).

Lie on the back with arms and legs straight. Turn the arms over so that the palms of the hands are facing upwards and the thumb is extended outwards (Figure 4.88).

Figure 4.88

Slowly move **the arms and legs** outwards. Take the legs as far as is comfortably possible, but continue with the arms in a circular motion until the two thumbs meet above the head.

Pause for five seconds (Figure 4.89).

Figure 4.89

Slowly return the arms and legs to the starting position (Figure 4.90).

Repeat the movement six times.

Figure 4.90

Slowly move **one arm only**, keeping the other arm and both legs still (Figure 4.91).

Repeat the movement six times.

Figure 4.91

Slowly move the **opposite arm only**, keeping the other arm and the legs still (Figure 4.92).

Repeat the movement six times.

Figure 4.92

Slowly move **one leg only**, keeping the other leg and both arms still (Figure 4.93).

Repeat six times.

Figure 4.93

[†] www.mlcscotland.com

Slowly move the **opposite leg only**, keeping the other leg and both arms still.

Repeat six times (Figure 4.94).

Figure 4.94

Slowly move **two arms together**, but keep the legs in the starting position (Figure 4.95).

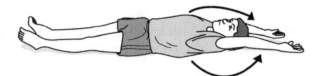

Figure 4.95

Repeat six times.

Slowly move the **two legs together**, but keep the arms still in the starting position (Figure 4.96).

Repeat six times.

Figure 4.96

Use the **right arm** and **right leg together**, keeping the left and leg still in the starting position (Figure 4.97).

Figure 4.97

Repeat six times.

Use the **left arm and left leg together**, keeping the right arm and right leg still in the starting position (Figure 4.98).

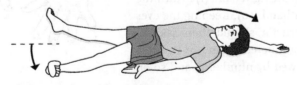

Figure 4.98

Use the **right arm** and **left leg together**, keeping the opposite arm and leg still in the starting position Figure 4.99).

Figure 4.99

Repeat six times.

Use the **left** arm and **right leg together**, keeping The opposite arm and leg still in the starting position (Figure 4.100).

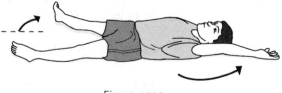

Figure 4.100

Repeat six times.

When all the above patterns have been mastered, alternate and randomise the different combinations above so that the child has to respond to changing verbal instructions.

If 'overflow' of movement is seen, that is the wrong arm(s) and leg(s) are also moving, return to the earlier pattern and give instructions more slowly.

If the child has difficulty following 'left' and 'right' in the early stages, use the instructions 'same side' and 'other side'.

4.3.2 FINGER EXERCISES

These are designed to improve manual dexterity, communication and inhibition of overflow movements between the two sides of the brain.

Start by asking the child to open and close clenched hands, initially both hands together and then one hand independently of the other. Alternate the movement between the two hands.

Ask the children to work in pairs.

One child should place his/her hands flat on a surface with the fingers spread out. The other child should touch different fingers on his/her partner's hand and ask him/her to raise the finger he/she has just touched (this can also be done with the eyes closed).

When this can be done easily, the fingers should be numbered 1 to 10, starting from the little finger of the right hand (1) to the little finger of the left hand (10). Keeping the **eyes closed**, the instructor should then ask the child to raise a numbered finger, for example number 4; followed by number 7; and so on (Figure 4.101).

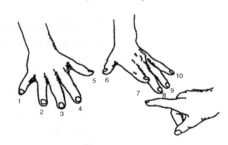

Figure 4.101

When the child is able to lift the correct finger in response to the numbered instruction, he/she is told to re-number the fingers from 1 to 10 starting with the little finger of the left hand (1) to the little finger of the right hand (10). Instruct the child to lift individual fingers according to numbered instructions as above.

Note: The additional exercises in this section should only be used as a supplement to the exercises in Section 4.2. They should never be used instead of Section 4.2. They will not be necessary for all children, but may be useful for those children who still have residual difficulties with fine muscle control and left/right discrimination.

▶ 4.4 POST SCRIPT

The exercises shown are suitable for use with children from six years of age.

If attempting to use with younger children, while children should be encouraged to carry out the movements as slowly and accurately as possible, children below the age of six can find this difficult.

To help young children perform the exercises slowly, a story 'Early Morning by the Pond' is available as an additional resource (Chapter 5).

Children aged between four and six years may find it easier to incorporate daily movements into a general play activity using song, stories and actions. 'Wings of Childhood' is a musical CD of songs and booklet with suggested movements designed as a less structured play activity for children aged 3–6 years (Chapter 5).

▶ REFERENCES

[1] Rowe, N (1996) Personal communication.
[2] Palmer, LL (1995) Readiness stimulation in pre-school and primary children (DVD). College of Education, Winona State University, Winona, MN.
[3] Dobie, S (1996) Exercises for bilateral integration. Paper presented at The European Conference of Neuro-Developmental Delay in Children with Specific Learning Difficulties, March 1996, Chester, UK.
[4] Dobie, S (2008) *Bilateral integration: The gateway to achievement*, 6th edn. Bilateral Exercise Integration Ltd, Balado, UK.

Resources

▶ TRAINING DVD

Access to video examples demonstrating all test positions, procedures, observations, scoring and individual exercises may be found by following the link www.accessnmr.inpp.org.uk. Registration on this page will give free access to the training DVD for one month.

▶ TRAINING

1. Additional one day training courses in the use of the INPP Screening Test and School Intervention Programme are held by INPP regularly throughout the year. For a list of forthcoming courses and international licensed course providers please visit www.inpp.org.uk.
2. For training courses in Bilateral Integration please visit http://www.mlcscotland.com/training.html.

▶ SUPPLEMENTARY RESOURCES

1. 'Early Morning by the Pond'. In: Goddard Blythe, SA (2004) The well balanced child. Hawthorn Press, Stroud, UK. Available from: orders@booksource.net or www.inpp.org.uk/ publications.
2. Music CD: Wings of Childhood – A CD of Nursery Rhymes for Modern Times.

This CD comprises bass and soprano voices intertwined with piano accompaniment. The songs are rendered in a wide range of sound frequencies. The second half of the CD repeats the songs removing the vocal parts and leaving the piano accompaniment for children to sing along or carry out movements.

The animal characters described in the songs evoke the principles of developmental movements – on land, in the sea and in the air. This is an ideal sound track for music and movement sessions. Children can crawl, run, skip, jump and roll, thus practising their own developmental movements and mirroring the movements of young animals experimenting with their own bodies.

Research has highlighted the significance of the child's listening environment in the pre-school years in acquiring the language skills – listening and speaking – which are necessary

Assessing Neuromotor Readiness for Learning: The INPP Developmental Screening Test and School Intervention Programme, First Edition. Sally Goddard Blythe.
© 2012 John Wiley & Sons, Ltd. Published 2012 by John Wiley & Sons, Ltd.

to support reading and writing later on. Singing along as a group activity helps to develop sound discrimination.

During the piano medley which follows the vocal songs, children may freely express the music with their bodies, using imagination to respond to the music. Props such as scarves and instruments can also be used.

The CD and booklet are the product of collaboration between Dr Michael Lazarev – a Russian paediatrician, musician and poet, head of children's rehabilitation (medicine) in Moscow, author of SONATAL (sound and birth) www.sonatal.ru – and Sally Goddard Blythe – Director of The Institute for Neuro-Physiological Psychology in Chester. The CD may be ordered from www.inpp.org.uk/publications.

▶ ADDITIONAL RESOURCES

SOUND THERAPIES

Auditory training programmes which can be carried out at home:

1. Johansen Individualised Auditory Stimulation (JIAST): www.johansenias.com
2. Listening Fitness Trainer (LiFT): www.listeningfitness.com
3. The Listening Program (TLP): www.thelisteningprogram.com

Auditory training programmes which must be supervised at a centre:

1. The Tomatis Method: www.tomatis.com
2. The Listening Centre (Madaule): www.listeningcentre.com
3. Auditory Integration Training (AIT): www.aitinstitute.org
4. Musica Medica: www.musicamedica.ch

▶ OTHER BOOKS BY THE AUTHOR

Goddard, SA (2002) *Reflexes, learning and behaviour*. Fern Ridge Press, Eugene, OR.
Goddard Blythe, SA (2004). *The well balanced child*. Hawthorn Press, Stroud.
Goddard Blythe, SA (2008) *What babies and children really need*. Hawthorn Press, Stroud.
Goddard Blythe, SA (2009) *Attention, balance and coordination – the A.B.C. of learning success*. John Wiley & Sons Ltd, Chichester.
Goddard Blythe, SA (2011) *The genius of natural childhood*. Hawthorn Press, Stroud.